THIS IS THE BOOK YOU GIVE YOUR

# DAD

EVERYTHING AN AWESOME FATHER WANTS TO KNOW

ILLUSTRATIONS BY **ANDREW JANIK**
TEXT BY **MATT GOULET**

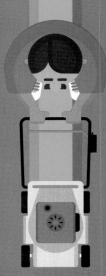

Simon & Schuster
1230 Avenue of the Americas
New York, NY 10020

First Simon & Schuster hardcover edition May 2019

SIMON & SCHUSTER and colophon are registered trademarks
of Simon & Schuster, Inc.

For information about special discounts for bulk purchases,
please contact Simon & Schuster Special Sales at 1-866-506-1949
or business@simonandschuster.com.

The Simon & Schuster Speakers Bureau can bring authors to your
live event. For more information or to book an event, contact
the Simon & Schuster Speakers Bureau at 1-866-248-3049
or visit our website at www.simonspeakers.com.

Manufactured in the United States of America

1   3   5   7   9   10   8   6   4   2

Library of Congress Cataloging-in-Publication Data is available.

ISBN 978-1-9821-0524-2
ISBN 978-1-9821-0526-6 (ebook)

# Dear Dad,

(WRITE SOMETHING NICE HERE!)

# CONTENTS

**Y**ou're a member of a special club, a covert alliance, a clandestine organization more shrouded in mystery than any college secret society or government spy agency.

That's right: you're a dad.

As such, you have a language all your own, a way of speaking and behaving that only other dads can understand, certain habits and rituals whose significance can only be appreciated by fellow fathers. And as all dads know, your kids are terrible at buying gifts. It's one of the first rules you learn when you're inducted into the club. No matter the occasion—Father's Day, your birthday, the holidays—they almost always wait until the last minute and botch it. You're a good sport. You smile and tell the kids they didn't need to get you anything, that the best gift you've ever received was them. But let's be honest: Wouldn't it be nice for once to get something you can enjoy? A keepsake that speaks to your select status in the fraternal order of fatherhood?

Well, here you go. A tribute to everything fathers love, all the passions and peculiarities that unite you. Your unreasonable fixation with lawn care and uncanny ability to identify classic cars. Your bad dancing and even worse jokes. Grilling and golf . . . of course, golf. It's all here. Part encyclopedia and part guidebook, fit for fathers old and new, *This Is the Book You Give Your Dad* is an acknowledgment of the special place you hold in the world. So kick back in the recliner, flip up that footrest, and bask in the awesomeness that is all things dad. You deserve it.

# THE HOME

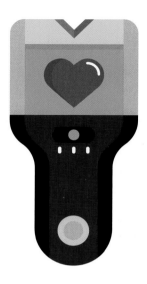

# THE STUD FINDER JOKE: NEVER GETS OLD

It is your God-given duty that should you find yourself holding an electric stud finder, you take said finder and place it against your person and press and release the button to emit an affirmative beep and say, "Found a stud right here." You certainly won't be the first to have made this joke, but you definitely won't be the last. And you'll be taking part in a great tradition of home DIYers.

## HOW TO > HANG A FRAME

**1**

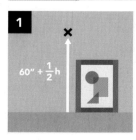

Paintings usually go up 60 inches high on a wall. Measure the length of your painting and divide it in half. Add that to 60 inches and measure it from the floor up. Mark that spot.

**2**

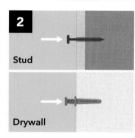

Stud

Drywall

Sink a large nail into a stud. Or if you're driving into drywall, drill a hole and install an anchored screw.

**3**

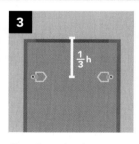

If you're using framing wire (usually for heavier paintings or mirrors), measure about 1/3 down from the top of the painting and install your eye hooks there.

**4**

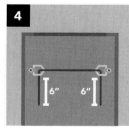

Thread the wire through the eye hooks, leaving about six extra inches of wire on each side to be threaded through and wound around the wire again for reinforcement.

**5**

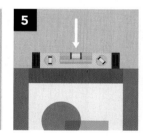

Bust out the leveler. The old-school version, not the app. Because few things in home repair are more gratifying than seeing that bubble perfectly centered.

# THE ESSENTIAL TOOLS OF A HANDY DAD

**Duct Tape**
When all else fails.

**Cordless Drill**
Always have a spare battery charged.

**Hand Saw**
Wipe WD-40 on it to prevent rust.

**Phillips-Head Screwdriver**
Large and small.

**Slip-Joint Pliers**
Allows a wide span, so you can get a grip on anything

**Tape Measure**
Use it twice, cut once.

**Claw Hammer**
Mind your fingers!

**Flat-Head Screwdriver**
Large and small.

**Wrench**
Get one with an adjustable head to fit any kind of nut.

**Socket and Ratchet Set**
The cure-all tool set for bike and toilet projects alike.

Build your own toolbox! See plans on page 25.

# MEDICINE CABINET ESSENTIALS

**Foot Spray**
For when the Gold Bond just isn't enough

**Gold Bond**
The most versatile item you can have. Powder your feet, your back, your undercarriage and stay dry and cool all day.

**Nail Clippers**
You want small, rounded ones for fingers, and a larger straight-edged pair for toes—to prevent ingrown nails.

**Nasal Spray**
Don't overdo it, but on a stuffy morning, a quick shot up the nose can rescue your day.

**Deodorant**
Do it like Grandpa did, and opt for the Old Spice.

**Shaving Cream**
Opt for a product that contains lanolin and oils, rather than the old foam, that helps plump up your whiskers, making them easier to shave.

**Eye Cream**
He also uses eye cream. A lifesaver to hide a hangover.

**Razor**
There is no dearth of options out there. Find the one that works for you, and replace the blade after every three shaves.

**Moisturizer**
Ever see a guy who's 65 and looks 45? He moisturizes.

Perhaps one of the more important skills you can pass down to your children, and it's not as gross as you think.

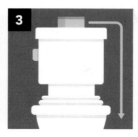
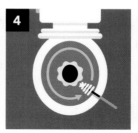

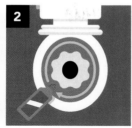

**1** First, for the love of all that is holy, flush the toilet, seat down. Then apply cleaner like Soft Scrub around the toilet bowl starting along the rim.

**2** Now tackle the outside. Working down from the tank lid, wipe down everything with the same cleaner, spending time on the handle and the exterior of the bowl.

**3** Spray and wipe down the seat, including inside the lid, under the hinges, and along the ledge of the bowl.

**4** Take a toilet brush that's been soaking in cleaner to the bowl. Like in basketball, attack the rim, scrubbing underneath the ledge where deposits build up, then the bowl, and finally the hole.

**5** Close the lid and flush.

# BATHROOM READING MATERIAL

For sanitary purposes, leave your phone out of the bathroom, please. And while a newspaper is a nice idea, the print tends to leave behind smudges on your newly sparkling porcelain (See: How to Clean a Toilet, above). A good magazine, preferably one with shorter articles, so your legs don't fall asleep, or stock up on a couple books of humorous essays from the likes of David Sedaris or Jean Shepherd (the guy behind *A Christmas Story*).

# FIX A RUNNY FAUCET

For a typical two-handled bathroom faucet, the good news is that this is easier to fix than you might think. Bad news: You'll need to do some hunting around the hardware store.

**1**

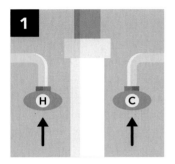

First, turn off the water from under the sink one feed at a time to determine which handle, hot or cold, is causing the leak.

**2**

Plug the drain in the sink. Remove the handle cap, and unscrew the handle revealing the valve stem assembly—the cause of your problem—and the nut holding it in place.

**3**

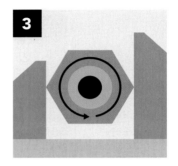

Using a wrench, remove the nut. Then unscrew and pry out the valve stem assembly by taking your pliers to the hex nut where the assembly meets the sink.

**4**

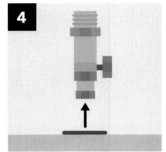

Now's the time for the field trip: Bring the whole assembly with you to the hardware store and pick up a replacement washer, which is held in place by a small screw at the bottom of the assembly.

**5**

You'll also want to pick up some plumber's grease and a replacement rubber O-ring.

**6**

When you're home, pry out the old, worn washer. Screw the new washer in place, and replace the O-ring, applying the plumber's grease around it.

**7**

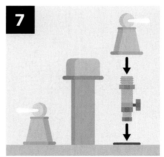

Reassemble the valve assembly and faucet handle.

**8**

You're back in no-drip action. Sleep soundly without that annoying noise.

# THE HARDWARE STORE OR HOME CENTER DECISION TREE

Should you go to your local hardware shop or the big box store?

START HERE

What is the nature of your project?

Quick, around-the-house repair

Building or installing something major

Are the kids in tow?

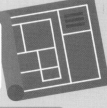

How long is your list?

Yes

No

Just a couple items

More than five items

Are the items you need common or hard to find?

Quality or Cost?

Hard to find

Common

Quality

Cost

OPEN

**HARDWARE STORE**

**HOME CENTER**

17

# LAWN EQUIPMENT ESSENTIALS

**Weed Wacker**
Wear protective glasses to keep your eyes safe from flying debris.

**Rake**
Even with a leaf blower, you still need a good old rake to catch the stragglers.

**Shovel**
A great lesson for kids in the drudgery of life: Make them dig a hole (see page 19).

**Sprinkler**
Do it in the morning for minimum evaporation.

**Leaf Blower**
Gas gets you more power. Electric is lighter. Choose based off the size of your lawn.

**Edger**
Like giving your lawn a haircut: it's not finished until you clean up around the ears.

**Fertilizer Spreader**
Just think: there was a time when this didn't exist and you had to use your hands.

**Hose**
It will get knotted. It will spring a leak. You will curse.

**Mower**
Want to be the star of your block? Get weird with the pattern (see page 20).

## THE SNOW SHOVEL

**FOSSILS OF FATHERHOOD**

There's something therapeutic about using a rake instead of a leaf blower. More control, less noise, calm repetition. But a snow shovel over a snowblower? Why risk a slipped disc, or worse, a heart attack? Why succumb to the cold? What's the virtue in digging yourself out of a snowed-in driveway with a piece of plastic when you can spew snow out of your way with a roaring engine? There's the kind of placid, quiet yard work that lets a dad ruminate while getting things done. And then there's the kind that's a toiling slog, like shoveling. The snowblower gives us a third kind of work all dads like: the get it done quick, easy, and before you freeze your heinie off kind.

## HOW TO ▶ DIG A HOLE

**1**
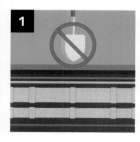
Check with your city and utility companies to make sure there aren't any pipes or wires where you're planning to break ground.

**2**
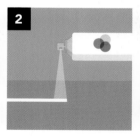
Outline the dimensions of your hole with white spray paint to act as a guide.

**3**

Break up the topsoil with a mattock or spade.

**4**
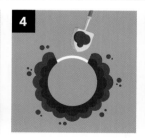
Dig out the perimeter of the hole first, then work your way in. It's all grunt work from there.

**5**
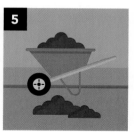
Save yourself cleanup by pitching the dirt onto a tarp laid out next to the hole or directly into a wheelbarrow.

# GREAT LAWN MOWING PATTERNS

**1** The simple back and forth.
Just go up and down.

**2** Create a diamond pattern by running diagonally over the lawn after having gone up and down as in step 1.

**3** Do steps 1 and 2. Then pick a diagonal light strip near the center of the lawn. Follow that then cut over 90 degrees to a dark strip, and back to the light. Continue this along the lawn to create a zigzag effect. It's a major-league move.

## WHEN A RIDER MOWER IS JUSTIFIED

If you're working on anything smaller than half an acre, getting a riding mower is a bit overboard. Consider a good propelled walk-behind mower, and thank yourself for the exercise. Or if you're lazy and have the means, get the rider!

**1**

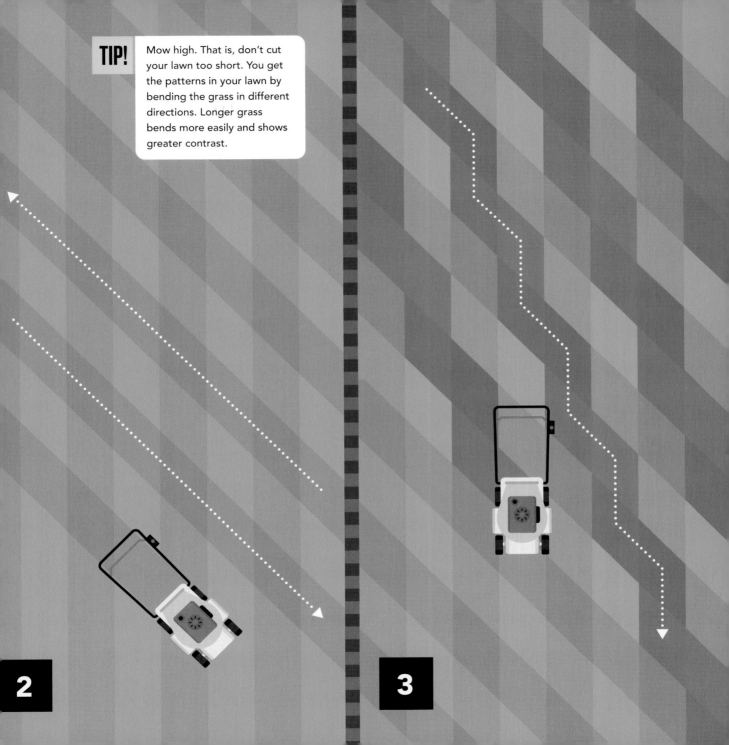

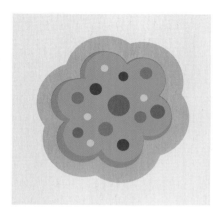

## PUKE

ON CARPET

1. Get out the plastic gloves.

2. Scoop up and remove as much of the vomit as you can.

3. Blot the area with a rag and dust the spot with baking soda, and let sit for 15 minutes.

4. Vacuum up the baking soda, then apply an enzyme-based cleaner like Resolve and blot with a dry rag.

5. Blot again with a clean, damp sponge or rag to rinse.

6. Blot with a dry rag to dry. And vacuum one more time once the spot is dry.

## BLOOD

ON TILE

1. Again, plastic gloves.

2. Wipe up as much as you can with paper towels and throw away.

3. Apply a 1:9 bleach solution to the area and let sit for 20 minutes.

4. Wipe up the solution with fresh paper towels or a clean rag.

5. Throw away the gloves and rags and paper towels into a single garbage bag and then double bag it.

## CRAYON

ON WALLPAPER

1. Wet a rag and apply a dab of dish soap to suds it up.

2. Wipe off the crayon with the rag. And then go over with a dry cloth or paper towel.

3. If that doesn't take it off, take a Magic Eraser or some WD-40 to the wall.

# MUD

## ON PAINTED WALLS

**1** Mix a gentle cleaner like dish soap or Murphy Oil Soap with water.

**2** Wipe down the wall with a sponge, from the top down.

**3** Then wet a rag with just water and wipe down again to rinse.

**4** Finally, wipe the wall dry with a dry cloth or paper towel.

# WHEN TO MAKE THE KID DO IT

A little effort early on to have them hang out while you're DIYing around the house can impart some basic skills. Before you know it you'll have a mini-handyman you pay in chicken nuggets.

## Age

 **5** A kid can start holding a tape measure as early as age 5.

 **8** Start them on the simple tedious things, like taping off a room you're preparing to paint, as early as 8, if they're precise enough.

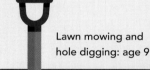 **9** Lawn mowing and hole digging: age 9

 **10** Hammers, drills, and saws are closer to age 10.

 **11** Cleaning the bathroom is around 10 or 11. They can Windex mirrors and windows well before then.

# THE BIRDHOUSE IN AN HOUR

| BACK | ROOF | SIDE | SIDE | FRONT | BASE |
|------|------|------|------|-------|------|
| 11" | 8 1/4" | 8" | 8" | 8" | 4" |

## MATERIALS

- One 4-foot-long piece of 1×6 lumber
- 16 nails

## INSTRUCTIONS

1. Mark off the individual sections on the pieces of wood and predrill drainage, ventilation, and house opening holes.

2. Cut your individual pieces of wood according to the measurements above and assemble with nails as directed.

3. Let two nails on one side act as a pivot for easy access for cleaning out the nest—should you ever actually consider doing so.

# THE TREEHOUSE
## IN A FEW (OR MORE) DAYS

## MATERIALS

- Two 2×10 pieces of lumber
- Two 6" or 8" lag screws
- Six 2×6 pieces of lumber, about 1½ feet long each
- 8 rafter ties
- 16 3" carpenter screws
- 40 4" deck screws
- 14 2×4 boards
- 32 nails
- 4 handrails (can be 2×4s)
- 36 square feet of siding (i.e., extra 2×4 boards, plywood, found wood, or mesh)
- Grips or ladder (optional)

# THE TOOLBOX IN A FEW HOURS

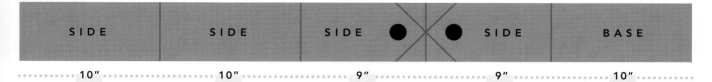

| SIDE | SIDE | SIDE | ● ✕ ● | SIDE | BASE |
|------|------|------|-------|------|------|
| 10" | 10" | 9" | | 9" | 10" |

## MATERIALS

- 1½"-wide wooden dowel, cut to 12"
- One 4-foot-long piece of 1x6 lumber
- 8 wood screws or nails

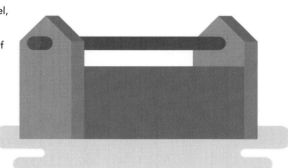

## INSTRUCTIONS

1. Measure and mark off your individual pieces of 1x6 as illustrated and cut. Drill a ½" hole on each triangular side panel for the dowel rod.

2. Line up the two rectangular side pieces with the base and screw or nail together. Next, align the triangular end pieces with the sides and base and secure with screws or nails.

3. Insert the dowel rod through the holes drilled into the peaks of the triangular end pieces.

4. Fill 'er up.

## FRAMING THE PLATFORM

1. Make sure the tree is stable, alive, and strong, with a trunk at least 20 inches in diameter.

2. Mount two 2x10 boards across the truck of the tree using 6" or 8" lag screws, to create support beams.

3. Lay 4 pieces of 2x6 perpendicular across the support beams, placing them on their sides and securing them with 3" screws.

4. Use two additional pieces of 2x6 to frame the base of your floor, securing the 2x6s to the support beams with rafter ties.

5. Cut the ends of 2 pieces of 2x4 at a 45-degree angle and brace them from the trunk of the tree to the inside edge of the platform.

## LAYING THE FLOOR AND INSTALLING THE RAILING

1. Use 4-inch deck screws to secure your floorboards to the frame. (Measure out where you'll need to cut around the trunk before trying to nail any boards in place.) Leave about quarter-inch between each board.

2. Nail 2 4-foot-high pieces of 2x4 uprights to each corner of the platform and screw them together. Nail the handrails to the uprights.

3. Install the siding between the handrails.

4. Install grips up the trunk, or build out the ladder, and get up there.

# HOW TO ⟩ PAINT A ROOM

## PREP FIRST:

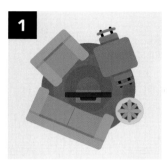

**1** Move the furniture out or to the center of the room and lay down drop cloths or tarps.

**2** Ready your surface by scraping off any loose, old paint, sanding down any high-gloss surfaces, and patching holes and cracks.

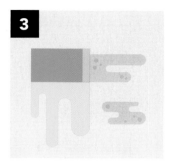

**3** Then clean the dust and dirt off the walls with a damp sponge.

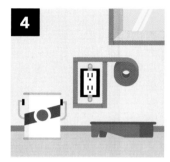

**4** Tape off the ceiling, remove the covers from and tape off any outlets, and tape along the molding at the floor.

## THEN PAINT:

**5** The general rule states that one gallon of paint will cover about 400 square feet, so buy enough paint based on your room's dimensions.

400FT²

**6** Cut in; that is, edge out the perimeter of a wall with a hand brush.

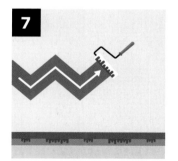

**7** Fill in the rest, going over the wall in a zigzag pattern, working from top to bottom, with a paint roller.

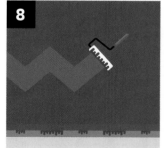

**8** Plan on going over everything in two coats. And if you're covering up a glossier paint, you'll need to do a coat of primer before you lay on the new paint.

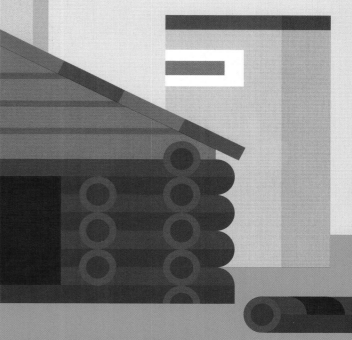

# THE WRIGHT STUFF

Being fired by his world-famous architect father might have been the best thing that happened to John Lloyd Wright, and generations of kids have benefitted from the family scuffle. The second born of Frank Lloyd Wright, the famous American arts-and-crafts style architect behind the Fallingwater house in Mill Run, Pennsylvania, and the Guggenheim Museum in New York City, had been employed by his dad's firm after himself becoming an architect. But a dispute of his pay led the younger Wright to strike out on his own. What John Lloyd Wright did in his now free time was to go on and create a classic American toy: Lincoln Logs. Using an interlocking wood design that his dad had developed for a hotel in Japan, John Lloyd Wright's toy has gone on to sell over 100 million sets. Sometimes, cutting the kids really can spur them to greatness.

# THE GREAT OUTDOORS

# ESSENTIAL DAD CAR CAMPING SUPPLIES

**Clothesline**
For clothes, yes, but also for stringing up that tarp.

See pages 44–45 for grilling tips.

**Tarp**
Stave off rain, create some shade. The most versatile item you can pack.

**Tent**
One dad and two kids don't really require an 8-person tent, but the extra room is a luxury.

**Sleeping Bag**
If you're going camping in mid-July, maybe don't bring one that stays warm 15 below zero.

**Lantern**
Electric works, but there's something to be said for the warm glow of a traditional gas lantern.

**Headlamp**
A flashlight on your head means you've got both hands free when night falls.

**Camp Stove**
Because cooking by fire alone is just too much work.

**Hot Dog Sticks**
Be they store-bought or foraged from the forest, make sure they're long and two-pronged.

**Cooler**
Drain the excess water throughout the day to avoid soggy provisions.

# HOW TO > SPLIT WOOD

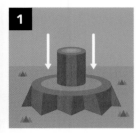
**1**

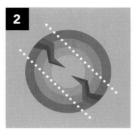
**2**

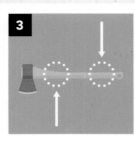
**3**

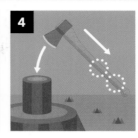
**4**

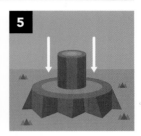
**5**

Set your preferably dry wood to be split on a large, sturdy stump —never on soft ground: it absorbs energy and is unstable.

Line yourself up with any cracks or seams already in the wood.

Plant your feet shoulder-width apart and hold the maul at your waist with one hand choked up under the head of the axe and the other at the far end of the axe.

Swing the axe over your head, letting your choked-up hand slide down the length of the handle as you swing down and through the wood.

Wipe the sweat off your brow with your shirtsleeve, bask in your handiwork for a moment…then do it all over again.

# HOW TO DEAL WITH CRITTERS

The best way to keep animals from intruding on your site and your enjoyment is to not attract them in the first place. Employ the clean-as-you-go method while you're at the site. Pick up trash as you make it. Don't burn any food or food packaging in the fire, as the smell will attract animals. If you're car camping, lock all your food, even coolers, and trash in the car at night. If the campground has bear bins, use them. And when you zip up the tent at night, make sure the zips are at the top of the door, not the bottom. Why make it easy for raccoons and their able hands?

# THE MAKE-AHEAD CAMPFIRE RECIPE: CHILI!

Planning is what takes a camping trip from bearable to great. A few days before you head out, make a pot of this chili and freeze it into blocks using Tupperware. Transfer the blocks to sealed Ziploc bags (better to double bag it), and store in the bottom of your cooler. On the second night of your trip, the blocks should have softened enough that you can easily warm the chili up in a Dutch oven over the fire. It's something hearty and feels outdoorsy, and is way more impressive than a hot dog—though, you shouldn't skimp on those.

## CAMP CHILI

**Ingredients:**

1 pound ground beef

1 cup chopped onion

½ cup chopped green bell pepper

1 clove garlic, minced

½ tsp cumin, 2 tbsp chili powder, or ½ package
   taco seasoning

One 28-ounce can diced tomatoes

One 15-ounce can tomato sauce

1 jalapeno pepper, diced

One 15-ounce can pinto beans, undrained

**Directions:**

1 In a large saucepan over medium-high heat, combine the ground beef, onion, and bell pepper. Sauté for about 5 minutes, or until beef is browned. Drain any excess fat.

2 Add garlic, cumin, tomatoes, tomato sauce, jalapeno peppers, and salt and pepper to taste. Bring to a boil. Reduce heat to low, and cover and simmer for 1½ hours, stirring occasionally.

3 Stir in the beans and heat through.

4 Let cool and freeze into blocks.

# HOW TO > BUILD A FIRE

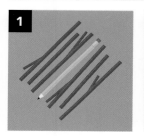
**1**
Gather tinder, no thicker than a pencil. Make sure it's extremely dry—it'll snap easily and noisily.

**2**
Light it from below and let it catch.

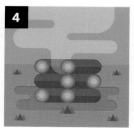
**3**
Add longer thumb-thick branches as kindling and let those catch from the tinder.

**4**
Build your larger logs around your roaring kindling—either in a teepee for a bigger bonfire or log-cabin style that'll burn down for good cooking.

**5**
Cue the s'mores and ghost stories.

# HOW TO > PUT OUT A FIRE

**1**
Let all the wood burn down to ash and embers.

**2**
Dump water onto the embers and stir the fire with a shovel to make sure they're all extinguished.

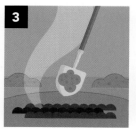
**3**
If you don't have water on hand, shovel sand or dirt onto the embers and stir.

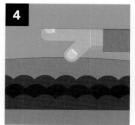
**4**
When it's cool to the touch, you're safe.

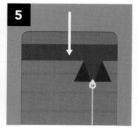
**5**
Hurry up and get in that sleeping bag!

# WORTH IDENTIFYING

EASILY!

## BIRCH

### IDENTIFYING DETAILS

White bark, often peeling, with horizontal gray stripes. Two- to three-inch-long oval-shaped leaves with serrated edges.

## GARLIC MUSTARD

### IDENTIFYING DETAILS

You want to know this one because it's an invasive species that needs to be controlled. When you find it, let a park ranger know. Single-stemmed plant with broad leaves and four-petaled white flowers. Smells like garlic when crushed.

## WHITE OAK

### IDENTIFYING DETAILS

The easiest way to tell a white oak from red oak is the leaves. The leaves of white oak are rounded and look almost like a white snowman. As opposed to the pointed leaves of a red oak.

## POISON IVY

### IDENTIFYING DETAILS

Climbing ivy, single plants, or bushes with leaves growing in clusters of three, usually with one large leaf at the stem's end, and two smaller ones below it, all with pointed ends.

## POISON SUMAC

### IDENTIFYING DETAILS

Red stems with seven to thirteen leaves growing in pairs, with a single leaf at the end. Long oval leaves, two-to-four-inches long.

# HAIRY WOODPECKER

Large bill. Black-and-white striping down the body. And a red band around the crown of the head. Causing all that racket.

# BLACK-CAPPED CHICKADEE

Small, compact bird. It has a black head with white cheeks and a gray back. You'll find it bouncing between branches and along pathways.

# BLUE JAY

It's blue, for starters. Note: it gets its name from the screechy *Jaaay Jaaay* call it makes.

# EUROPEAN STARLING

Common bird with black and purple-green iridescent feathers and yellow bill. Makes many different calls, often imitating other species of birds.

# RED-TAILED HAWK

A mostly pale underside with a dark band around the belly and along the wing tips. White and brown throat.

# TURKEY VULTURE

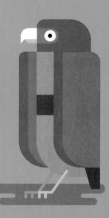

Easily confused for a red-tailed hawk. Look for a white outline around the wings, a boxy, rectangular wing shape, and a wobbly flight pattern.

## THE COMPASS

## THE FOLDING MAP

# FOSSILS OF FATHERHOOD

Once, there was planning. Days, weeks even, before a trip, the compass would be unearthed and maps would be spread out on the kitchen table, a highlighter tracing your route, points of interest jotted down, mileage accounted for, notes from last year's trip cross-checked. Then, the map would be folded up—usually on the third attempt after mismatching the creases on the first two tries—and slipped in the glove box or in the console, at the ready. Or slipped into a Ziploc bag and stuffed into a backpack for the trail. Now, there is the phone and the backup battery. And just a little bit more spontaneity.

# THE HILLARYS AND THE MOUNTAIN

Sir Edmund Hillary and Tenzing Norgay became the first people to summit Mount Everest in May 1953. About a year and a half later, Hillary's son, Peter, was born. The kid spent his childhood following along on his dad's expeditions, learning to climb mountains like a pro himself. In 1990, Peter Edmund Hillary summited Everest, 47 years after his dad. The two became the first father-son duo to have reached the world's highest peak. Not to be outdone by his dad, Peter visited the mountain five more times, summitting twice in total.

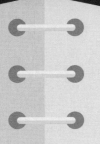

1953

1990

# HOW TO > CLEAN A FISH

**1**

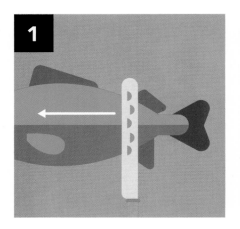

Scale the fish by laying it down so the head faces your nondominant hand, and hold it there. Run a butter knife in short, quick strokes from the tail to gills. Flip over, scale the other side of the fish, and rinse.

**2**

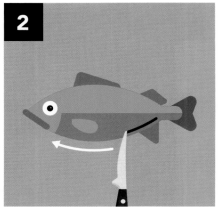

Insert the tip of a fillet knife into the anus of the fish, near the tail. Draw the blade along the belly, up to the head. Make sure to keep just the tip of the knife in the fish, and don't cut too deep.

**3**

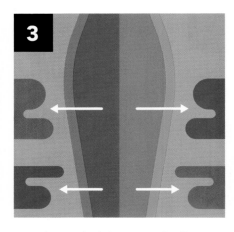

Spread open the fish cavity and pull out the entrails. Cut out the anus in a V-shape. Scrape out with a spoon any kidneys or other organs.

**4**

With a gentle but firm stream of water, rinse out the inside and skin of the fish.

**5**

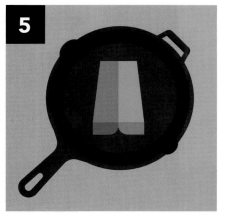

Cut off the head, if it's a pan fish. Leave the head on if it's trout. And cook or fillet as you see fit.

Learn how to clean your cast iron pan on page 47.

# THE
# LURE TO FRESHWATER FISH
## INDEX

When you want to reel them in like a pro, it helps to think beyond the balled-up pieces of bread.

THE LURE

THE FISH

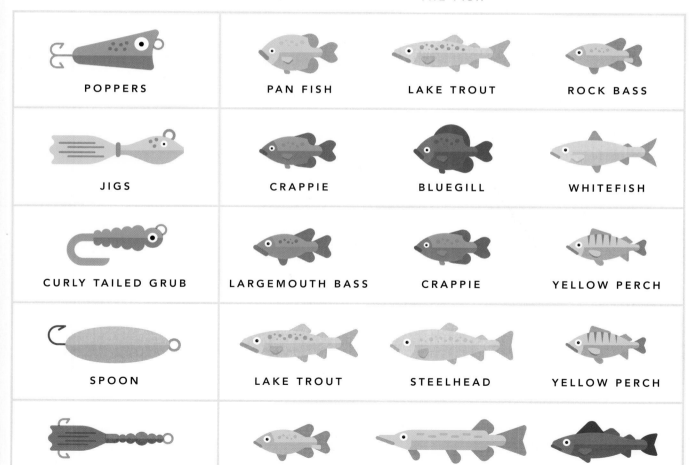

| THE LURE | THE FISH | | |
| --- | --- | --- | --- |
| POPPERS | PAN FISH | LAKE TROUT | ROCK BASS |
| JIGS | CRAPPIE | BLUEGILL | WHITEFISH |
| CURLY TAILED GRUB | LARGEMOUTH BASS | CRAPPIE | YELLOW PERCH |
| SPOON | LAKE TROUT | STEELHEAD | YELLOW PERCH |
| SMALL SPINNERS | ROCK BASS | PIKE | WALLEYE |

# BEACH DAY ESSENTIALS

**Umbrella**
Make sure it's secure. You don't want to be the dad chasing it down the beach.

**Beach Blanket or Straw Mat**
Keeps your setup tidy and not too sandy.

**Sunscreen**
Apply early and often.

**Book**
Leave the Tolstoy for the library. Beach reads should be light and easy.

THIS IS THE BOOK YOU GIVE YOUR DAD

**Cooler**
See opposite page for how to pack

**Proper Beach Chair**
That is, one that reclines—for prime tanning angles.

**Bluetooth Speaker**
Unless you're on a private island, keep the volume reasonable.

**Beach Towel**
The bigger and burlier, the better.

# HOW TO > PACK A COOLER

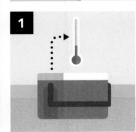
**1**

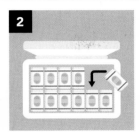
**2**

**3**

**4**

**5**

First, temper your cooler: throw some ice in the cooler and close it up to bring down the internal temperature. Let it sit for an hour or so. Then dump it out.

Start with a layer of fresh ice to coat the bottom of the cooler. Then put down a layer of cans, laying them on their sides. Make as tight a layer as possible.

Dump in another layer of ice, making sure it moves into the gaps between cans.

Continue with another layer of cans, then set in any snacks you'll want to keep cool.

Throw in a final layer of ice, again moving it around to fall between your items.

# THE JOY OF TOSSING A KID AROUND THE WATER

Kids are some of the most easily impressed people on earth. Also the lightest. So what a great way to show off your inherent strength by chucking a 58-pound goofball across the five-foot-deep part of the pool or into a wave. It's like you get to become a human version of Splash Mountain—feels just a little dangerous, but it's all good, family fun.

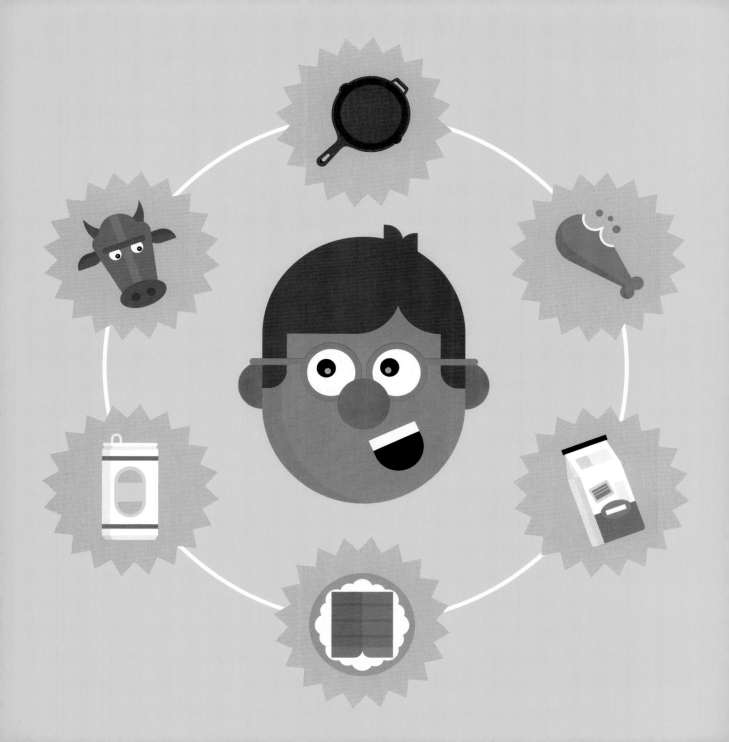

# FOOD AND DRINK

# CHARCOAL OR GAS?

There's a purity to charcoal that hearkens back to the ancestral roots of cooking over fire, and fire emanating from burning wood. The smell of lump charcoal imbues its own flavor in your food. And the process of getting things lit and hot is a ritual, or a total pain in the ass, depending on your point of view. Opt for gas if you want quick, clean eating. Just know, some consider it cheating.

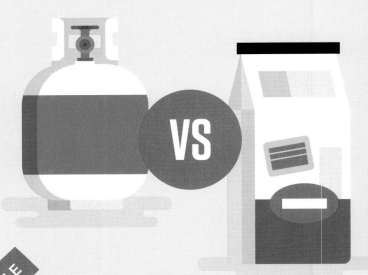

VS

TEST ZONE

## HOW TO KNOW WHEN YOU'RE GRILL IS HOT ENOUGH

If your grill doesn't have a thermometer or, more likely, your grill's thermometer is broken, hold your hand two or three inches above the grill grates. If you can only keep your hand there for three or four seconds before it feels like you might be charring your palm, your grill is hot enough to sear.

## THE GRILL

## IS IT DONE?

Use your palms. That is, a rare to medium-rare piece of steak will give and feel fleshy like the meaty part below your thumb. Just above that is well-done.

WELL-DONE

MEDIUM

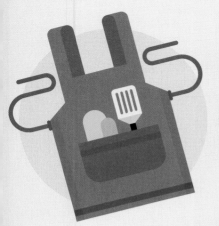

## TO WEAR OR NOT TO WEAR THE APRON

Not as an added layer of protection, but as a layer of context. People know you're the man in charge of this whole operation, and you've got a sense of humor about it. "Kiss the Cook" is an ageless aphorism.

For tailgating tips, turn to pages 80–81.

## THE CHARCOAL CHIMNEY

It's not so much lazy dad as genius dad. Invest 12 bucks in a charcoal chimney that lets you get a fire ripping and ready to grill with the ease of lighting a match and without the fireball risk of excess lighter fluid. Just stuff the bottom with newspaper to get a flame going. Fill with charcoal and light. Then dump it out onto your grill when the flames start licking out over the top of the chimney.

# GRILLING VEGETABLES

First, do it. All the time. Second, if you're going to do it all the time, invest in a grill pan. Spare yourself losing stray pieces of asparagus between grates or over-scorching pieces of zucchini by keeping everything in the pan, that will still sear the veggies and imbue them with some char. Finally, do it with lettuce, too. Slice a head of romaine in half lengthwise and set on the grill. Veggies always take less time to cook than you think you need.

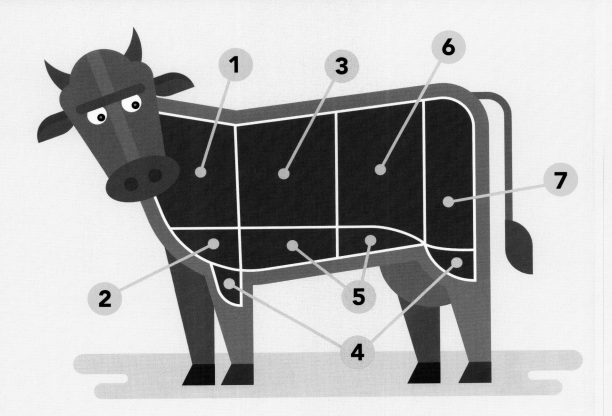

# CUTS OF BEEF

**1** **Chuck** $
From the shoulder of the cow, the meat tends to be tough but flavorful, which is why you'll often find it ground for hamburgers, or in beef stew wheres it's cooked down until tender.

**2** **Brisket** $$
Cut from the front breast, it's a fatty meat that's best for low and slow cooking like barbecue or corned beef.

**3** **Rib** $
The back section of the cow's ribs— the front set of ribs are included in the chuck—is where you'll find tender, marbled meat for cowboy steaks, rib eyes, and Delmonico steaks.

**4** **Shank** $$
Tough meat that's found at the top of the forearm, just below the brisket, and the back leg. Use it for stews and soups.

**5** **Plate/Flank** $$
The lower cut of the rib cage, closer to the bottom of the cow, loaded with fatty meat and good flank steak.

**6** **Loins** $$$
The money spot. The prime (and often most expensive) cuts come from just near the back of the cow.

**7** **Round** $
The back end of the cow tends to get a lot of work, resulting in a tougher, leaner (and cheaper) piece of meat. Use a top round cut for roast beef, cooking it low and slow for a tender finished product.

**1**

After cooking, wash the pan by hand, scraping out any large bits first.

**2**

Put a tablespoon of kosher salt in the pan and add a little water. Scrub off any other bits by hand.

**3**

Rinse and dry thoroughly with paper towels.

**4**

While the pan is still warm; rub it with a light layer of oil like vegetable oil.

**5**

If you really need to, use a small amount of dish soap on the pan. But be sure to apply oil again afterward.

# IF YOU'VE GOT A RUSTED PAN . . .

Re-season it by scrubbing off the rust with a metal scrub brush. Wash it clean, apply a layer of cooking oil to all sides of the pan, and bake it upside down in an oven for one hour at 350 degrees F. Let it cool in the oven.

# THE PERIODIC TABLE OF BEER

## THE ALES
Known for their top-fermented method, where the yeast gathers and turns to alcohol at the top of the vessel at high temps. Also known for full-bodied taste and hoppiness.

### BA
**BROWN ALE**

Medium bodied with a nutty, sweet flavor and less hops. (i.e., Newcastle)

### PA
**PALE ALE**

Golden colored with a hoppy flavor. (i.e., Sierra Nevada)

### IPA
**INDIA PALE ALE**

Ales with a higher alcohol content and a stronger hop flavoring. (i.e., Lagunitas Brewing Co. IPA)

### PT
**PORTER**

Ale brewed with roasted malt, which imbues it with a dark color and slightly bitter flavor. (i.e., Founder's Porter)

### ST
**STOUT**

Ale brewed with roasted barley, which give it its creamy head and dark flavor. (i.e., Guinness)

### WH
**WHEAT**

German beer made from at least 50% wheat malt (as opposed to barley). Known for a cloudy appearance and light color. (i.e., Allagash White)

### HF
**HEFEWEIZEN**

Wheat beer with strong yeasty flavor. (i.e., Paulaner)

BEER

# THE LAGERS

Brewed so that yeast sinks and is fermented at the bottom of the brewing vessel and at colder temperatures. Known for crisp, lighter-tasting beer.

## AL
**AMBER**

Brewed with more malt than other lagers to give it a darker amber color. (i.e., Yuengling)

## PL
**PILSNER**

From Czechoslovakia, brewed with more hops for a crisper flavor and medium body. (i.e., Pilsner Urquell)

## BK
**BOCK**

Fuller bodied with a dark brown color, brewed with more malt. (i.e., Shiner Bock)

## DL
**DOMESTIC LIGHT**

Usually brewed with cheaper, substitute grain, for lower alcohol content and an all-American taste. (i.e., Bud Light)

# CHOOSING THE RIGHT GLASS

Having the right glass to pour your drink into can be just as important as your beer selection.

Domestic Lights     Pale Ale, India Pale Ale, Porter, Stout     Lagers such as Pilsners and Domestic Lights, Wheat Beer     Just about anything     You guessed it, IPAs

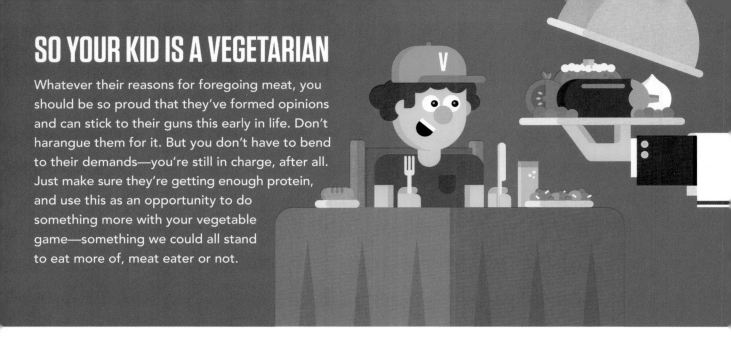

# SO YOUR KID IS A VEGETARIAN

Whatever their reasons for foregoing meat, you should be so proud that they've formed opinions and can stick to their guns this early in life. Don't harangue them for it. But you don't have to bend to their demands—you're still in charge, after all. Just make sure they're getting enough protein, and use this as an opportunity to do something more with your vegetable game—something we could all stand to eat more of, meat eater or not.

## THE THREE-MARTINI LUNCH

FOSSILS OF FATHERHOOD

The three-martini lunch was once a comfortable reality for the corporate dad thanks to reasonably sized portions of booze and the time in a workday to luxuriate at a table where gin-fueled business dealings led to chitchat which led to the really good ideas. Thanks to the march toward optimization and, well, overall health, the three- or even one-martini lunch has all but disappeared. To what end? No one's ever made the deal of a century over a desk salad.

# HOW TO > CARVE A TURKEY

**1**

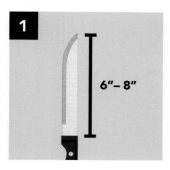

Use a six- to eight-inch knife to slice between the body and the leg, moving down toward the joint where they meet.

**2**

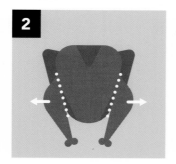

Use your hand to crack the joint and break off the thigh and drumstick. Remove both legs.

**3**

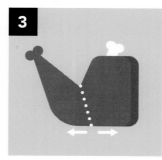

On each leg, slice through the V-shaped part where the drumstick and thigh meet and pull them apart.

**4**

Remove the thigh bone by running your knife along both sides of it, and twisting it out of the meat of the thigh.

**5**

Pull the wing away from the body of the turkey, and slice through the V-shaped point where the body and wing connect like you did with the leg. Remove both wings.

**6**

Remove each breast by running your knife down along the rib bone of the turkey, pulling the meat away as you go.

**7**

Lay the breast flat on your cutting board and slice—against the grain of the meat—into individual pieces about a quarter-inch thick.

**8**

Be sure to save a drumstick for yourself. You've earned it.

# HOW TO

 # DRINK WHISKEY

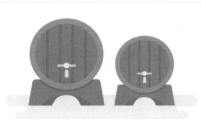

## 1 KNOW WHAT YOU'RE DRINKING

Whiskey is a spirit distilled from grains like wheat, barley, corn, and rye and aged in oak barrels (that's where a lot of the flavor and coloring comes from).

**STATESIDE** **INTERNATIONAL**

### Bourbon

Bourbon is made with at least 51% corn and aged in charred oak barrels, and is at least 80 proof when it's out of the barrel. (Like Maker's Mark or Jim Beam)

### Rye

Rye whiskey is made from a mash that's at least 51% rye. (Like Knob Creek Rye)

### Tennessee

Tennessee whiskey is charcoal filtered and, you guessed, made solely within Tennessee's borders. (Like Jack Daniel's)

### Malt

Malt whiskey is made with at least 51% malted barley. (Like Woodford Reserve Straight Malt)

### Scotch

Scotch whisky is made in Scotland and tends to have smokier or peatier notes. (like Johnnie Walker)

### Others

Irish whiskey (like Jameson), Canadian whisky (Crown Royal), and Japanese whisky (Yamazaki)—yes, there are different spellings—each have different barreling requirements.

# 2 NOW THE ACTUAL DRINKING

If you're drinking it neat, you'd do well to add a drop or two of water to release flavors and aroma from the booze. You can also add one large ice cube to do the same and slightly dilute the drink more.

**NEAT** + **WATER** OR **ICE** = **DELICIOUS**

If you're going for appreciation, note the color and texture of the liquid. Swirl it in the glass and let the aroma hit your nose before the drink makes it to your lips. Note what you smell: vanilla, caramel, smoke, oak. Then sip, almost chew on the liquid, tasting the different flavors from the spirit.

# 3 MAKE A COCKTAIL

## OLD-FASHIONED

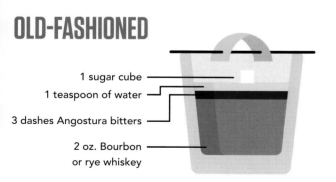

1 sugar cube

1 teaspoon of water

3 dashes Angostura bitters

2 oz. Bourbon or rye whiskey

In a rocks glass, add the sugar, bitters, and water and muddle so the sugar dissolves. Add three ice cubes to the glass and stir. Add the whiskey and stir again. Twist a lemon or orange peel over the drink for garnish.

## MANHATTAN

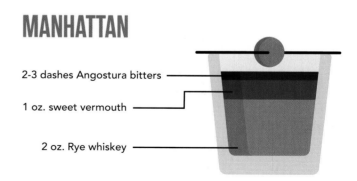

2-3 dashes Angostura bitters

1 oz. sweet vermouth

2 oz. Rye whiskey

Add the rye, vermouth, and bitters into a mixing glass with ice and stir to combine. Strain into a chilled glass and garnish with a maraschino cherry.

# THE APPETIZING DAD-DAUGHTER SHOP

Joel Russ was an immigrant from what is modern-day Poland when he began selling schmaltz herring in 1907 in New York's Lower East Side. The pushcart became a storefront, and the storefront became a bigger storefront by 1920. He needed help running the shop, and so he enlisted his daughters Hattie, Ida, and Anne. By 1935, he'd made his three daughters (Joel didn't have any sons) full partners in the family business and changed the name to Russ & Daughters. It's widely believed to be the first business in the country to have an "& Daughters" in its name. The shop is still run by the fourth generation of Russ family members out of the 1920 Houston Street location, selling smoked fish, caviar, desserts, dips, nuts, and dried fruits.

# WHAT SHOULD
# ALWAYS BE IN THE FRIDGE

**1  Jar of Olives**
For martinis or impromptu party spreads.

**2  Cold Cuts**
Sandwiches, sure, but also for doctoring-up a frozen cheese pizza.

**3  Seltzer**
None of the sugar of soda, all of the bubbly fun.

**4  Backup Sixer**
For unexpected guests. Or after a particularly rough day at work.

**5  Leftovers**
What's in the Tupperware? Not sure. How long has it been in the fridge? Can't say. Nope, you're not tossing it.

**6  Cheese Sticks**
There is not a whining child who cannot be placated with a well-timed cheese stick.

**7  Jelly**
Not jam. Not marmalade. Not preserves. Jelly.

**8  Mayonnaise**
The best-selling American brand Hellman's started as a New York delicatessen in 1913.

**9  Mustard**
Dijon for vinaigrettes and salad dressings. Yellow for late-night sandwiches and hot dogs.

**10  Eggs**
Scrambled, hard-boiled, poached: as long as you have eggs, you have a meal.

**11  Bottle of White Wine**
For drinking and cooking. Mostly drinking.

# PANCAKES

## INGREDIENTS

- 1½ cups all-purpose flour
- 1 teaspoon baking powder
- 2 tablespoons sugar
- ½ teaspoon salt
- 1¼ cups whole milk
- 2 eggs
- 2 tablespoons butter, melted, or 2 tablespoons vegetable oil
- 2 teaspoons butter, or oil, for cooking
- Optional: blueberries, chopped strawberries, chocolate chips

## DIRECTIONS

1. In a large mixing bowl, whisk together flour, baking powder, sugar, and salt.

2. Make a well in the flour mixture and pour in milk. Crack in each egg and add 2 tablespoons melted butter. Mix to combine; it's okay if there are lumps.

3. Heat a griddle over medium heat, and melt 2 teaspoons butter or oil. When butter foam subsides or oil shimmers, ladle batter onto griddle. Here's where you can drop in some blueberries, strawberries, or chocolate chips if you want to take your pancakes to an 11.

4. When bubbles begin to appear on the face-up side (2 to 4 minutes), flip the pancakes and cook until lightly browned on both sides.

5. You can keep your stack warm by transferring the cooked pancakes to a plate and putting them in an oven set to 200 degrees F.

# SALAMI ROLLS

## INGREDIENTS

- ½ pound Genoa or hard salami
- Mustard to taste

## DIRECTIONS

By the light of the fridge, remove Genoa or hard salami from its deli counter plastic. Peel off one piece of salami at a time, squirt a line of mustard down the middle of the slice, and roll. Consume. Repeat as desired.

# SHEET-PAN SALMON

Serves 4

## INGREDIENTS

- 4 salmon fillets, 5 to 6 oz. each
- ½ pound green beans
- Olive oil, to taste
- Salt and pepper, to taste
- Juice of 1 lemon

## DIRECTIONS

1. Preheat the oven to 425 degrees F.

2. Lay the fillets in the middle of a sheet pan lined with aluminum foil. Arrange the green beans around the fillets. Drizzle with olive oil and season with salt and pepper, and toss to coat. Pour the lemon juice over everything.

3. Bake for 10 to 15 minutes, or until the salmon is no longer pink and shiny, but still tender.

# CHICKEN SALAD SANDWICHES

Serves 6

## INGREDIENTS

- 3 cups cooked chicken, shredded (grocery store rotisserie chicken works well for this)
- ¾ cup diced celery
- ¾ cup mayonnaise
- 1 teaspoon celery salt
- ½ teaspoon dried dill
- ½ teaspoon dried parsley
- Salt and pepper, to taste
- Rolls or croissants, for serving

## DIRECTIONS

1. In a large bowl, combine shredded chicken, celery, mayonnaise, celery salt (the secret ingredient!), dill, and parsley. Mix everything together, and add salt and pepper to taste.

2. Cover and refrigerate for an hour. Serve the chicken salad on a roll or croissant, or eat it straight out of the bowl.

# FOUR GO-TO RECIPES

Even the most kitchen-averse dad can master these.

# ENTERTAINMENT

# YES, PLAYING VIDEO GAMES WITH THE KIDS IS QUALITY TIME

Sometimes it's raining or snowing. Or the lawn has just been reseeded. Or sometimes you just don't want to go outside. You can still engage in competition with the kids by playing video games. The time spent is just as valid if it's on the couch as opposed to in the front yard. Because if you're working together to take out enemies on Fortnite, or trying to outsprint each other on FIFA, or riffing over each other on Guitar Hero, the lessons about sportsmanship and teamwork and—we may be stretching it a little here—hand-eye coordination are just as valid. Just make sure it's age appropriate. Father-child time playing Grand Theft Auto is uncomfortable and confusing for everyone.

Remember the VCR? When watching a movie, let alone recording a playoff game, required something that felt like a skill? A skill that fit squarely in the domain of Dad: futzing with the tracking, adding a two-minute window on either side of a recorded program, precisely timing when to let your thumb off the fast-forward button, fishing tape out of a jammed seven-inch-wide, one-inch-tall metal slit. It wasn't much, but the VCR was a place a dad could flex some technical muscle. Today, a four-year-old and a dad can both easily tell Siri to play the latest episode of *Mickey Mouse Clubhouse*. Fathers today have traded a sense of capability for convenience.

## THE VCR

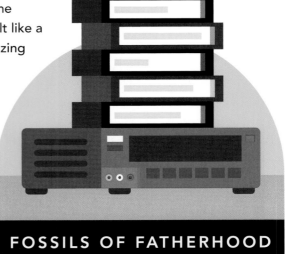

**FOSSILS OF FATHERHOOD**

## YOUR CHAIR

That feeling when you walk into a room and there's a space carved out, waiting for you. Where the cushioning has adapted to your contours. In it, you occupy a space where you feel wholly yourself, completely comfortable. A place from which you can quiet down or orate to a rapt audience. Every king needs a throne. Be it worn leather or a spot at the head of the dining table, it's a place from which you can rule with benevolence and perspective.

## THE POWER OF THE POWER NAP

Say you've got a busy Saturday lined up around the house—some yard work, a project in the basement, lots on the to-do list. Come 3 p.m., you find yourself flagging a bit. Rather than brewing a midday pot of coffee, consider power napping. Fifteen minutes in a sunny spot on the living room floor, like the dog does. Lie down, close your eyes, quietly recharge, and then get back out there.

"The key to fathering is don't overthink. Cause overthinking is . . . um, what were we talking about?"

**HOMER SIMPSON**
*The Simpsons*

"Son, I'm going to show you how the world really works. I'm going to take your wallet, kick you to the ground, and punch you in the gut."

**HANK HILL**
*King of the Hill*

"You know who's really good to talk to about stuff? Your mother."

**TONY SOPRANO**
*The Sopranos*

"What's small potatoes to some folks can be mighty important to others."

**ANDY TAYLOR**
*The Andy Griffith Show*

THE TIMELESS
# WISDOM OF
# TV DADS

"If you love something, set it free. Unless it's a tiger."

**PHIL DUNPHY**
*Modern Family*

"As you go through life, try to improve yourself—not prove yourself."

**WARD CLEAVER**
*Leave It to Beaver*

"Nobody does anything without help. People opened doors for me, and I've worked hard to open doors for you. It doesn't make you any less of a man to walk through them."

**PHILLIP BANKS**
*The Fresh Prince of Bel-Air*

"Now that you're taking on a job, you're taking on a responsibility. Be prompt, hard-working, and loyal."

**MIKE BRADY**
*The Brady Bunch*

"If you're wondering if a boy is thinking about you, he's not. He's thinking about sex or he's hungry. Those are the only two options."

**ERIC TAYLOR**
*Friday Night Lights*

# "LUKE, I AM YOUR FATHER"

Darth Vader has just lopped off Luke Skywalker's hand and pushed him to the ledge of some outer space scaffolding. The guy is hanging on for dear life (one-handed!) when Vader decides to tell him, "Oh, by the way, I'm your dad, we should do something together sometime." It's a fatherly move—push kids to the edge, letting them get as far as they can on their own, then trying to help them out.

# THE HI-FI SETUP

Bluetooth speakers are great for the beach and tailgaiting. But all dads know that when listening to music at home, you need a *real* sound system.

# 1 RECEIVER OR AMP

For pushing your signal through to your speakers from your source. A receiver has a built-in AM/FM broadcast receiver, if you plan on playing the radio through your sound system. More important, it has Wi-Fi or Bluetooth for digital streaming. If that's not a priority for you, or you plan on playing only vinyl, go for a smaller-sized amp.

# 2 SPEAKERS

If you're going with a passive setup (hence the amp), aim for high-frequency, low-watt speakers with a sensitivity over 90 decibels. Opt for a subwoofer; two front-facing speakers; and if you're going for surround sound, two rear-facing speakers. Powered speakers take direct input from your music source and don't require a receiver.

# 3 OUTPUT

If you're still playing CDs, go with a combo Blu-ray–CD player. And then there's the cool dad option: a vinyl turntable.

# 4 ARRANGEMENT

If everything's relatively close, use 16-gauge audio wire to connect your receiver to your speakers. The speakers should be as far apart from each other as they are from the space where you'll be doing most of your listening (the couch), so the speakers and you form an equilateral triangle.

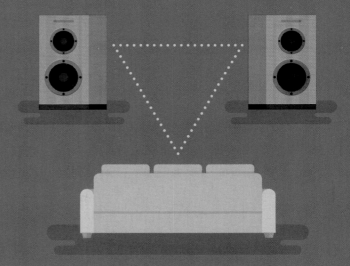

### THE ODE:
## CAT'S IN THE CRADLE

Harry Chapin's 1974 classic cuts to the core of fatherhood. What you want to give your kids. What they want from you. The fleetingness of time and how every moment is ripe for trauma or triumph. The importance of milestones like witnessing their first steps and teaching them to toss a ball. The necessity of appreciating the present. It's all here in four tear-jerking minutes.

# THE BEST WORST DAD JOKES

An old couple is driving down I-75 when the wife gets a call from their daughter.

"Mom, there's a car going in the wrong direction on I-75 near your house!"

The wife turns to her husband, who's driving, and relays their daughter's call.

"Did you hear that, some lunatic is driving down the wrong side of the freeway!"

The husband says, "One lunatic? There's hundreds of 'em!"

A little girl walks into a pet shop and asks in a lisp, "Excuthe me, mither, do you have wittle wabbits?"

The shopkeeper, delighted by the little girl replies, "Would you like a wittle white wabbit or a fuzzy bwack wabbit?"

The girl leans forward and tells the shopkeeper, "I really don't fink my pyfon giveths a thit."

Did you hear about the truck of Viagra that'd been hijacked? Police say to be on the lookout for hardened criminals.

Two cannibals are eating dinner when one says to the other, "I really hate my sister."

The other cannibal replies, "Well, just eat the noodles."

A man helps a drunk up at a bar and offers to take him home. On the way to the car, the drunk falls down. So the man helps him back up again. Three times this happens. As they walk up to his house, the drunk falls down. So the man helps him back up again. Three more times this happens. Finally, the man rings the bell and tells the drunk's wife, "Here's your husband!"

"That's great," the wife says, "but where's his wheelchair?"

A woman rushes into her home one morning and says to her husband, "Jack, pack up your stuff. I've just won the lottery."

"Should I pack for warm weather or cold?" he asks.

"Whatever," she tells him. "So long as you're out of the house by noon."

A guy sees an empty seat at the Stanley Cup finals. He asks the guy next to it why it's empty, and he says, "It was my wife's, but she died."

The guy asks, "Couldn't you have brought a friend?"

The guy in the seat replies, "They're all at the funeral."

A man races into a bar, sweating and shaken. He shouts to the bar's patrons:

"Does anyone own a six-foot penguin? Does anyone own a six-foot penguin?!"

All the patrons shake their heads.

The guy says, "Damn, I hit a nun."

# KNOW YOUR BONDS, JAMES BONDS

## 7 FILMS

### SEAN CONNERY

DEFINITIVE BOND GIRL
Pussy Galore

FIERCEST VILLAIN
Goldfinger

> I think he got the point.

KILLER ONE-LINER
(after harpooning henchman)

COOLEST GADGET
Jet Pack

## 1 FILM

### GEORGE LAZENBY

DEFINITIVE BOND GIRL
Tracy Di Vicenzo

FIERCEST VILLAIN
Blofeld

> He had lots of guts.

KILLER ONE-LINER
(after skiing henchman chopped up in snow plow)

COOLEST GADGET
Radioactive Lint

## 6 FILMS

### ROGER MOORE

DEFINITIVE BOND GIRL
Octopussy

FIERCEST VILLAIN
Jaws

> He always did have an inflated opinion of himself.

KILLER ONE-LINER
(after forcing henchman to swallow a compressed gas pellet and watching him explode)

COOLEST GADGET
Submarine Lotus

1960          1970          1980

## 2 FILMS

### TIMOTHY DALTON

**DEFINITIVE BOND GIRL**
Pam Bouvier

**FIERCEST VILLAIN**
Franz Sanchez

> He got the boot.

**KILLER ONE-LINER**
(after cutting off shoe and sending henchman falling to his death)

**COOLEST GADGET**
Rocket Launcher Boom Box

## 4 FILMS

### PIERCE BROSNAN

**DEFINITIVE BOND GIRL**
Jinx Johnson

**FIERCEST VILLAIN**
Alec Trevelyan

> They'll print anything these days.

**KILLER ONE-LINER**
(after henchman crushed in newspaper press)

**COOLEST GADGET**
Flamethrower Bagpipe

## 4 FILMS (and counting?)

### DANIEL CRAIG

**DEFINITIVE BOND GIRL**
Vesper Lynd

**FIERCEST VILLAIN**
Raoul Silva

> Doesn't time fly.

**KILLER ONE-LINER**
(cuing love interest to throw exploding watch at henchmen)

**COOLEST GADGET**
Palm-identifying Pistol

1990     2000     2010     2020

# CARS

# THE
# FAMILY CAR SELECTOR

## THE MINIVAN

For the family open to the complete embrace and ownership of being a brood. Drives like a cloud, plenty of room. What's not to love?

## THE CROSSOVER

It's the modern minivan for people who don't want to own up to driving a minivan. Deceptively small cargo space.

# THE SUV

Playing the long game, with a ride that can fit the family, get you out into nature, and be used to move kids and their stuff to college.

# THE TRUCK

Slightly impractical. Yet still spacious. Flies in the face of other dads who couldn't convince their wives to get on board with putting the kids in a pickup.

# THE SEDAN

For families of an only child.

# HOW TO > FIX A FLAT IN THE MODERN AGE

## THE BAD NEWS

Most cars these days don't even come with a spare tire (in an effort to reduce weight and emissions). Instead, you'll often find a repair or patch kit and a set of run-flat tires.

## THE GOOD NEWS

Those run-flat tires! Even without any air in them, a pair of run-flat tires can get you about 50 miles, which should (hopefully) be close to a service station. If you're worried about making it, or whether your tires could handle a blowout, it's wise to drop your own spare into your trunk.

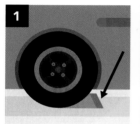

**1** Make sure the car is in park. Brace a tire that will stay on the ground with a piece of wood.

**2** Place the jack in the correct position. This varies car to car, and the best points can be found in your owner's manual.

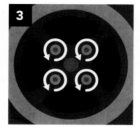

**3** Before you raise the car, loosen the lug nuts on the wheel with a tire wrench.

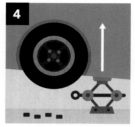

**4** Jack up the car, remove the lug nuts, and pull the wheel off the hub.

**5** Slide your spare, or your repaired tire, onto the wheel hub.

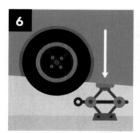

**6** Thread the lug nuts back on tightly, then lower the car with the jack.

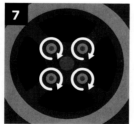

**7** With the wheel back on the crown, tighten the nuts one more time with a lug wrench.

**8** Then roll on over to the service station.

**FOR THE LAZY DAD**

1. Take out your phone.
2. Call AAA.
3. Play the waiting game.

# A WIN FOR NUMBER THREE

Beloved Hall of Fame NASCAR driver Dale Earnhardt died in a tragic crash on the final lap of the Daytona 500 in February 2001. The absence of his No. 3 car was felt, when, in July that same year, Earnhardt's son Dale Earnhardt Jr. returned to the Daytona International Speedway—the Pepsi 400. Dale Jr. had been on the track, leading his father, on the day of the crash. Now, not even six months later, and his season floundering amidst the family tragedy, his No. 8 car took the lead at Daytona and claimed the win.

# SEVEN

# ESSENTIAL CLASSIC CARS

EVERY DAD SHOULD KNOW

## 1950s

### '59  CADILLAC COUPE DE VILLE

The first generation of the classic Cadillac nameplate sported the iconic extra-tall tail fins on the rear that made it look like a rocket ship on the road.

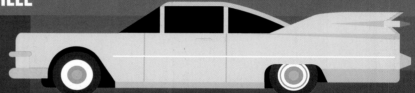

## 1960s

### '69  CHEVY CORVETTE STINGRAY

The sales brochure for this third-generation Corvette, with its wider stance and bevy of gauges and lights, touted that it had a gauge "for everything but your blood pressure."

## 1970s

### '73  PORSCHE CARERRA 2.7RS

This iteration of Porsche's 911 iconic bubble design is considered one of the greatest of all time. The 210-horsepower engine helps, too.

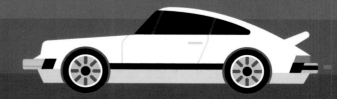

## 1980s

### '84 DeLOREAN DMC-12S

If only for the gull-wing doors and its pop-culture bonafides, the DeLorean is forever imprinted on the memory of dads the world over. With or without a flux capacitator.

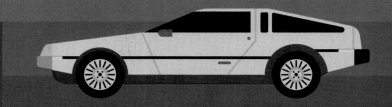

## 1990s

### '92 DODGE VIPER

Part of the new wave of American performance cars, the RT/10 had British roadster roots, in that it went without outside door handles to reduce wind drag.

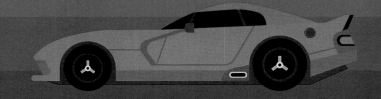

## 2000s

### '05 FIFTH-GENERATION MUSTANG

A complete rehash of the classic reinvigorated the American muscle car look for a new generation with a boxy design, and clocked 0 to 60 in 7.3 seconds.

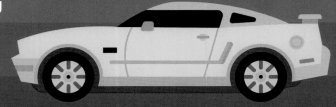

## 2010s

### '15 TESLA MODEL S

The first fully electric luxury car that made plug-in driving a reality in the minds of car lovers and regular drivers alike. It can go 335 miles on a single charge, according to the EPA.

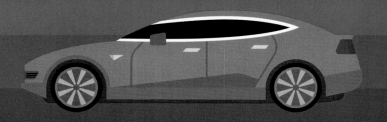

# HOW TO ▸ WASH A CAR

**1**

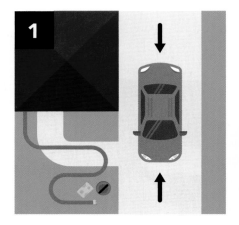

Pull the car into the middle of the drive, far enough down so your neighbors can see what a great Saturday you're having. Fill up a five-gallon bucket with a solution of car wash soap and water.

**2**

Hose the car from the top down, taking a moment to spray the kid.

**3**

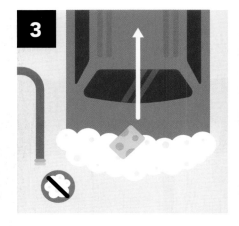

Working from the car roof down and in sections from back to front, use a sponge to lather the surface, and rinse as you go.

**4**

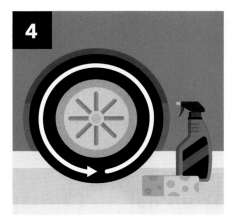

Save the tires for last, working between the rims, and using a tire cleaner on the rubber.

**5**

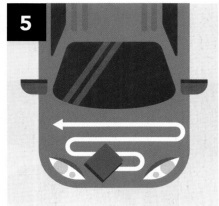

Wipe dry with a chamois rag.

**6**

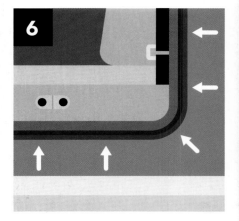

Don't forget to open the doors and wipe down the doorjambs.

# THE DRIVE-IN

Used to be, you'd load up the station wagon with the kids, pull up in the gravel lot with the big white screen, and take in a flick from the comfort of your roomy family vehicle. Back when cars were the size of living rooms. Now drive-in movies have become more like drive-*around*, with each kid tuned into the entertainment on their respective device as you shuttle them about. You're not really watching together anymore, but the car ride is much more peaceful. It's not a lament. Just an acknowledgment of a shift. Drive-ins still exist, though, and the novelty of watching a movie through the windshield is a memory the kids are sure to cherish.

## THE ODE:
## FIELD OF DREAMS

You think it's a movie about baseball and the ghosts of the game, and James Earl Jones delivering a poetic monologue about the game and America. But once those ghosts recede back into the corn, and the sun sets over Iowa, there's just Kevin Costner as Ray Kinsella and one lingering ghost, his father. And you realize, oh, baseball is a conduit. It's not the legendary players and their myths that make America's pastime special. It's the quiet, redeeming exchange that happens as father and child, no matter how old, fall into the hypnotic rhythm of a catch.

# TAILGATING

## A CONVERGENCE OF DAD WORLDS

Where cars, food and drink, the great outdoors, and sports collide.

**Collapsible Canopy**
Because all that beer doesn't mix well with direct sunlight.

**Pee-Wee Sized football**
Easy to grip and send sailing across a parking lot without denting cars.

**Chips**
Dump them in a bowl. All those grubby hands reaching in the bag is just gross.

**Lawn Chairs**
Serious tailgaters go for the kind with the built-in drink holder. But beach chairs will suffice.

**Beer**
Preferably, domestic light. Preferably, icy cold.

**Bluetooth Speaker**
Tune to the local pre-game show and steal analysis you can pass off as your own.

**Garbage Bags**
Extra large and heavy duty. Nothing kills the game-day vibe like leaking food juice.

**Cornhole Set**
See page 94 for how to sink a bag.

**Portable Propane Grill**
Make sure to always pack extra gas. You will use more than you think.

## PREPARE

If the big game's Saturday, plan your menu by the Tuesday before. Grocery shop and stock up on essentials like snacks and beer Thursday night. Do your prep Friday night—marinating and skewering kabobs, wiping out the cooler, and packing up your utensils. Also, pack up what you can in the car.

## SET UP

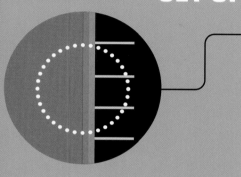

If you're doing this right, you'll have downed half a thermos of coffee and arrived as soon as the parking lot opens, or shortly thereafter. Try to find a spot on the perimeter of the lot that abuts grass or open space, so you're not tailgating in the back of someone else's tailgate. First, set up your canopy. (You brought a canopy, right?) Then, set up your cooking space and where you'll be laying out your spread. It's a small gesture, but putting the chips in a bowl makes a tailgate look about 115% more professional.

## COOK AND DRINK

If it's an early game, add some schnapps or whiskey to that coffee. Or bloody Marys and beer. But pace yourself. You've got to pack this all up and actually watch a sporting event eventually. Bring things out in waves so it feels like a party. Put out the snacks, like veggies and dip, first. Then present the big pot of meatballs you've been working on.

## THE EMPTIES GESTURE

If you're in an environment that condones it, carefully separate your empty cans from the trash and put them in their own bag for local collectors to pick up and cash in. Consider it a donation for swooping in on a swath of the city for the day.

# SPORTS

# EXPECTATION CHART

The best ages for kids to get the basics down.

You can help kids with their motor skills by having them step forward with the foot opposite their throwing hand. Emphasize distance over accuracy so they work the full range of motion.

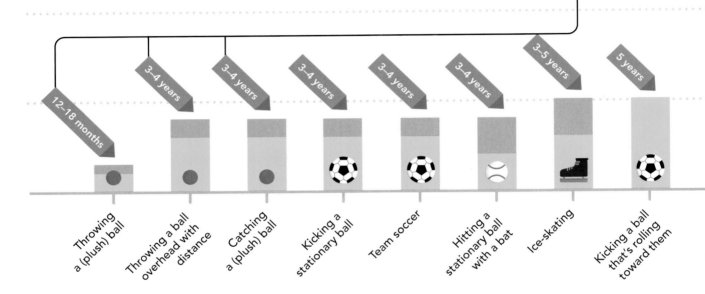

12–18 months — Throwing a (plush) ball

3–4 years — Throwing a ball overhead with distance

3–4 years — Catching a (plush) ball

3–4 years — Kicking a stationary ball

3–4 years — Team soccer

3–4 years — Hitting a stationary ball with a bat

3–5 years — Ice-skating

5 years — Kicking a ball that's rolling toward them

# WHEN TO STOP LETTING THEM WIN

2702
DAD    KID

You don't want to raise a quitter. Helping along little victories early on when playing with your kids encourages sportsmanship, but so does coping with losing. As a toddler, they're not even focused on winning or losing. Around five or six, though, when they begin to focus on the competition aspect of a game, you should let them win some and lose some. Each time, show by example what a good winner and a good loser looks like. If you've built a solid enough competitor, there will come a day when they'll beat you outright, without you having to hedge. And if you've taught them well, you'll be able to handle the loss.

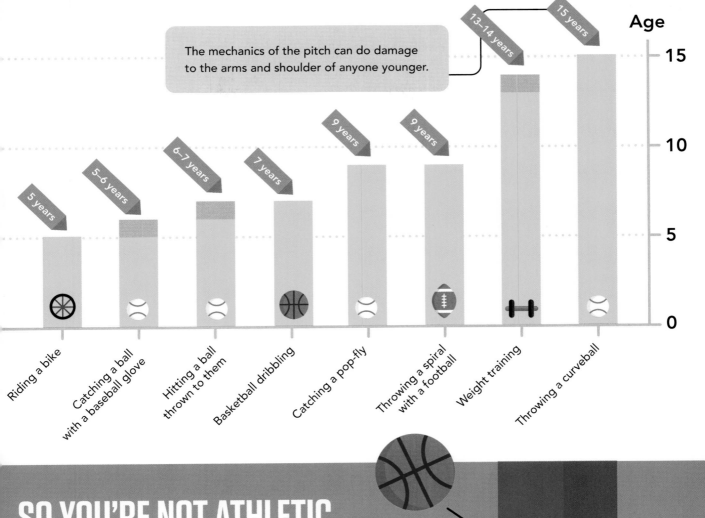

**Age**

The mechanics of the pitch can do damage to the arms and shoulder of anyone younger.

- 5 years — Riding a bike
- 5–6 years — Catching a ball with a baseball glove
- 6–7 years — Hitting a ball thrown to them
- 7 years — Basketball dribbling
- 9 years — Catching a pop-fly
- 9 years — Throwing a spiral with a football
- 13–14 years — Weight training
- 15 years — Throwing a curveball

# SO YOU'RE NOT ATHLETIC

Your kid is running, jumping, catching, kicking, and throwing like some kind of prodigy. Meanwhile, you're lucky if you can land a jumper from inside the paint. You're not athletic. That's okay. As long as you can handle the basics—you can catch a ball lobbed by a kid, and you can toss it back to them—they'll think you're LeBron James himself. Once they get into youth sports, let the coaches help develop their skills, and you do your part by encouraging them from the sidelines and making sure they're a good sport.

# THE ANNOTATED
# SIDELINE DAD

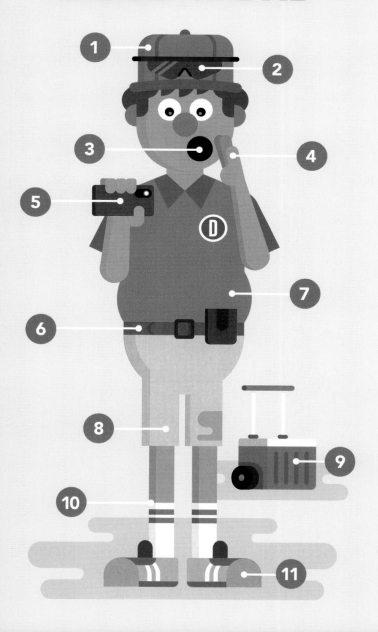

**1** Hat
Team logo. Or most well-worn local pro team.

**2** Sunglasses
Wraparounds. Lenses may be reflective.

**3** Mouth
Shouting words of encouragement or coaching to his child. Or making passive-aggressive remarks about the umpire or ref.

**4** Hands
Either in an aggressive clapping motion, or framing the mouth like a megaphone, or holding a phone out.

**5** Phone
Capturing frame-by-frame action or complete video of mundane little league sports action.

**6** Belt
Brown dress belt. May include a cell phone belt clip.

**7** Shirt
Tucked in. Either a T-shirt or polo emblazoned with the team logo.

**8** Shorts
Hitting right at the knee. Knee may have grass on it, from kneeling to console a small player.

**9** Cooler
Telescoping handle, wheeled. Filled with orange slices for after-game snacks.

**10** Socks
White, pulled to mid-calf.

**11** Shoes
Sports sneakers in near pristine condition.

# CONFOUNDING
# SPORTS RULES EXPLAINED

 **HOCKEY** > **OFFSIDES**

Offsides is called when any player on the team in possession of the puck crosses the blue line into the opposite team's defensive zone before the puck does. In other words, the puck has to cross the line that delineates the area between the goal and the net before any player on the team attacking the net can enter. Hockey's a fast-moving game, so offsides can happen quick, which is often why you're wondering what the hell just happened.

 **BASEBALL** > **THE GROUND RULE DOUBLE**

When two bases are awarded to a batter by an umpire because what was a fair ball became unplayable due to the ballpark's "ground rules"—as in the rules of the grounds. The classic example is when a ball gets stuck in the ivy at Wrigley Field. That's an automatic ground rule double, and all baserunners advance two bases.

 **BASKETBALL** > **DEFENSIVE THREE SECONDS**

Once a player on offense crosses half-court with the ball, any defensive player within the paint (that is, the area between the baseline and the free-throw line) has to be actively guarding an offensive player within three seconds. The rule is meant to keep defensive players from just standing in the paint, guarding the net instead of players. An active guard position means being within an arm's length of an offensive player. If a defensive player steps away from the player he's guarding for more than three seconds, the ref calls the violation and the offense is awarded a free throw.

 **SOCCER** > **OUT OF BOUNDS**

Unlike football or basketball where the line itself counts as out of bounds, for a ball to have gone out of bounds in soccer it has to have completely crossed the goal or touchline. A ball still counts as in play even if it's on the line, or if it bounces off a crossbar, flag, or referee.

 **FOOTBALL** > **THE CATCH RULE**

This one was new for the 2018 NFL season as an attempt to get rid of confusion. Jury's out on whether it's only exacerbated it. A catch in the NFL is now defined by three elements. First, control of the ball (it's in the player's hands or arms before it touches the ground). Second, a player in control of the ball touches the ground in bounds with either both feet or any part of his body other than his hands. And finally, once he's in control of the ball, and both feet—or another part of the body—touch the ground, he performs a "football move" like tucking the ball away, taking an extra step, or extending the ball forward. Now, you've finally, officially completed a catch.

 **GOLF** > **FLAGSTICK ATTENDANCE**

Say you're chipping or putting from just off the green, with another player on the green close enough to the flag to touch it. Even though they don't, that still counts as attending the flag, and if your ball hits the flag, you're penalized two strokes. It's a rule plenty of non-pro golfers break without knowing it.

# HELP YOUR KID PICK A TEAM

## ACCOUNT FOR GEOGRAPHY

If you're lucky, you and your kid occupy the same physical vicinity. And if you're luckier, there's a nearby pro sports team, where you guys can go to games and build a shared affection for the team's triumphs and losses, together.

## CONSIDER YOUR OWN LOYALTIES

Maybe you grew up a Browns fan but have moved out of Ohio. Do you really want to subject your child to that same level of suffering and still be hundreds of miles away from the team? Maybe. Could be good for their character. But don't force it. They'll naturally get on board with whoever you're rooting for when they're younger. Putting them in the gear of your favorite team before they can dress themselves helps.

## LET A SUPERSTAR BE THE GUIDE

It's hard to compete with a star player that commands the national stage. Live in Denver and your kid's asking for a Bryce Harper jersey for their birthday? You might be at a loss. But try learning some of the more commanding presences on your local or loyal team and get your kid excited about the athletes they can see do amazing things nearby.

GRIFFEY SR.

30

GRIFFEY JR.

24

GREAT MOMENTS IN DAD HISTORY

D

## THE GRIFFEYS

Ken Griffey, Jr. was twenty years old in 1990, and had just made his first All-Star Game appearance as a Seattle Mariner. His father, Ken Griffey, Sr., was a 41-year-old utility player for the Cincinnati Reds facing imminent retirement. But before hanging up his spikes, he signed with Seattle. On August 31, 1990, the father and son duo took on the Kansas City Royals, batting second and third in the lineup, respectively. While the rest of us are resolved to cherish our front yard games of catch, the Griffeys, on September 14, 1990, hit back-to-back home runs in the major leagues.

# GOLF

## WHAT IS IT?

Eighteen or 9 holes, each with a varying par or number of strokes determined by the course that the best golfer would take to get his ball from the tee to the pin. Your goal is to do just that: get your match or beat par. You're playing mostly against yourself and the environmental elements, manmade or otherwise. You're also playing against your ability to get a 1.5-oz. white ball into a hole several hundred yards away.

18

18 | PAR
4

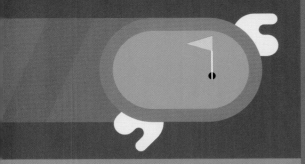

# OK, BUT WHY?

How did quietly walking around on varyingly manicured lawns and ripping a ball with a metal stick become the de facto dad sport? The answer is partly in the question: quiet and lawns. Plus, equipment and courses that can vary from the most basic to extremely advanced. Throw in an athletic element—though not too athletic—and you've got the ultimately fatherly leisure respite.

**FORE!**

## GOLFING WITH YOUR GROWN CHILDREN IS ADULT CATCH

You likely don't share a front yard to toss a ball around in anymore. So what better way to catch up with your kids than a round of golf? Over the course of an afternoon, you can small talk, share what's going on with your lives, or keep quiet and simply relish the increasingly rare opportunity to be in each other's company. However, resist the urge to analyze their swing or offer putting pointers. They're not children anymore. If they hit a bad shot, keep the critiques to yourself.

**FOR THE** ZZZ **LAZY DAD**

Always take the golf cart.

# FIX YOUR SLICE

More often, your ball is veering off to the side because you're hitting it with an open club face. Some combination of your grip and the steepness and angle of your swing is preventing you from having the face of the club come into straight, closed contact.

### CHECK YOUR GRIP

With a soft grip—not too tight—your hands should be turned away from your target, and your palms should be facing each other, rather than crossing over each other. Turn your left hand around the club until you can see three knuckles.

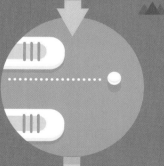

### BALL POSITION

You might be coming at the ball wrong, because the ball isn't in the best spot. Make sure that from your stance, the ball is just inside of your left foot (if you're right-handed).

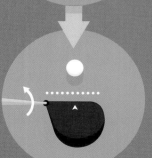

### RELEASE THE CLUB

Not like let it go midway through swing, but let your hands roll over each other just as you make contact. This will square up the club face before you hit the ball.

# THE FRUSTRATION INDEX

The appropriate reactions to golf's most infuriating humiliations.

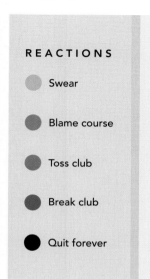

**REACTIONS**

- Swear
- Blame course
- Toss club
- Break club
- Quit forever

| HUMILIATION | REACTION SEQUENCE |
|---|---|
| SLICE | ●●● |
| WATER HAZARD | ●●●●● |
| LOST BALL | ●●●●● |
| BADLY MISSED PUTT | ●●●●●● |
| STUCK IN SAND TRAP | ●●●●●●●● |
| SLOW PLAY AHEAD | ●●●●●●● |
| GOOSE ATTACK | ●●●●●●●●● |

---

## HOW TO  >  SINK A THREE-FOOT PUTT

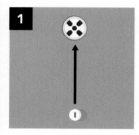

**1**
Aim your ball. That is, line the ball up from the markings on it in the direction you want it to go toward the hole, taking into account any breaks in the ground.

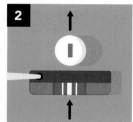

**2**
Now that the ball is aimed up, find that line with your club. The face of your club should be directly square to it.

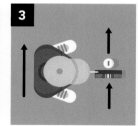

**3**
Next, line your body and shoulders square to the putter. You want everything to be on straight, square lines. It's physics.

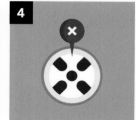

**4**
Finally, aim small. Pick a singular point in the back of the cup you want to direct the ball to. The hole in general is too large of an area and opens you up to error.

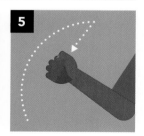

**5**
Deploy Tiger Woods's fist pump or Chi Chi Rodríguez's sword routine.

# BEER-DRINKING SPORTS SKILLS

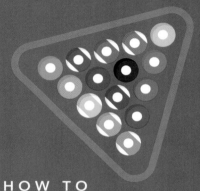

## HOW TO
# BREAK IN POOL

1. Like bowling a strike, aim for the pocket between the first and second rows of balls.

2. Set the cue ball off to the left or right of center, so you can lean on the rail for better aim.

3. Keep the cue stick level. Line up square to the cue ball, about a half inch below center—You don't want to add any spin here.

4. Move your hips forward on your follow-through for greater force.

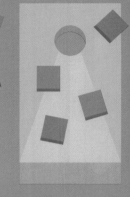

## HOW TO
# SINK A BAG IN CORNHOLE

1. Grip the bag toward the top of your palm, squeezing the top with your thumb and three ringers below and with your index finger along the corner seam.

2. Step forward with your leg opposite your throwing arm and launch the bag with an underhand toss, releasing at about 40 degrees.

3. Aim for the back of the hole and, using your index finger grip, put a spin on the bag on release.

4. On your follow-through, your fingers should be pointing at the back of the hole, where your bag has (hopefully) slipped through.

# HOW TO
# THROW A BULL'S-EYE

**1** Point your toe in a straight line toward the target. Keep your bicep straight and horizontal to the ground, and your forearm perpendicular. Keep your arm straight on your back swing, and keep it as close to your body as possible.

**2** Hold the dart with a light grip, with your thumb and index finger holding the back of the dart, while your middle finger steadies the point.

**3** Keeping your arm and bicep straight, make your throw, releasing about two thirds into the throw, just as your forearm crosses the perpendicular line to the ground. Finish so your finger is pointing straight at the bull's-eye. Where your dart should be.

# HOW TO
# BOWL A STRIKE

**1** You want the ball to strike the pocket— the sweet spot between the first and third pins if you're a right-handed bowler. And between the first and second pins if you're left-handed. To get there, use the arrows on the lane to guide your aim. You want the ball to follow the first arrow right of center, for right-handed bowlers.

**2** Keep your arm straight on your back swing, and keep it as close to your body as possible.

**3** Release the ball at the bottom of your swing downward, and add a slight spin to it by letting your hand roll over the ball. On your follow-through, have your hand continue to rise up in a pendulum motion, as if the ball were still attached to you.

# TEXAS HOLD 'EM

More likely, when you're talking about playing poker with friends, you're talking about playing Texas Hold 'Em. Here are the basics.

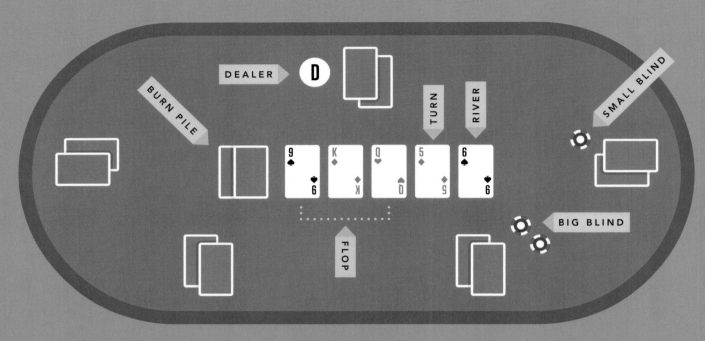

**1** Two players to the dealer's left post the blinds, a set dollar amount to kick off the game.

**2** Each player is dealt two cards. Everyone bets based off those two cards, either calling, raising, or folding, starting with the player who posted the smaller blind.

**3** Then the dealer flips over three cards in the middle of the table—The Flop. Players use these to build their hands off what they're holding. Then the players bet again.

**4** The dealer burns a card at the top of the pile by turning it facedown. Then he flips over the fourth card—The Turn. Another round of bets, either calling, raising, or folding.

**5** Then the dealer burns another card. Then flips over a fifth—The River.

**6** The players still in build a five-card hand based on any combination of the common cards that have been turned over and the two in their hand.

**7** A final round of bets. Then the players show their hands. Whoever has the highest-ranking hand takes the pot.

WINNER

THREE OF A KIND

TWO PAIR

# HAND RANKINGS
Just like Yahtzee. The winningest hands, from high to low.

### ROYAL FLUSH
A sequence of the face cards and 10, all of the same suit.

### STRAIGHT FLUSH
A sequence of five cards in the same suit.

### FOUR OF A KIND
Four cards of the same rank.

### FULL HOUSE
Three matching cards of one rank, and two of another.

### FLUSH
Five cards of the same suit, but in no order.

### STRAIGHT
A sequence of five cards in different suits.

### THREE OF A KIND
Three cards of the same rank.

### TWO PAIR
Two sets of two cards of the same rank.

### ONE PAIR
One set of two cards of the same rank.

### HIGH CARD
The highest-ranked card in a hand where there is no other sequence, matching rank, or suit.

# HOW TO ▶ HOST POKER NIGHT

**1**
Have enough chips—both poker and the edible kind.

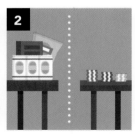

**2**
Set the snacks up on a table separate from the game. You don't want to crowd the table with Cheetos dust.

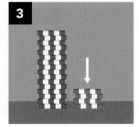

**3**
Remember that you set the tone, so if this is a casual, all-in-good-fun game, keep it light and the stakes low.

**4**
Establish the house rules at the outset.

**5**
Finally, coasters.

# STYLE

### The Oxford

In classic blue or white, collared button-down. And if it fits right the seams of the arms hit right at your shoulders.

### The Suit

Navy or charcoal, and your go-to for any and all formal events—weddings to funerals and everything in between. Use a wooden hanger with broad shoulders to help retain shape.

### The Sweatshirt

An oversized cotton crewneck of the college you either went to or the college you want your kids to go to. Often worn over a polo or oxford shirt.

# INSIDE THE DAD CLOSET

### A Classic Sneaker

Your Chuck Taylor, your Stan Smith— the more classic the style, the more it can do.

### Wing Tips

Dresses up jeans or makes a statement with a navy suit.

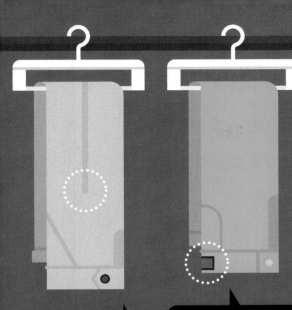

### The Khakis

A shade too light and likely pleated, single or double. The improved pair: they're in a darker English khaki color with a flat front.

### The Jeans

The old dad jeans were stone-washed, high-waised, wide-legged ... and godawful. These days, thankfully, they are dark-wash, mid-rise, and slim-legged.

### The Sweater

Probably V-neck, probably too big. And in an itchy wool. Improve it by sizing truer to your regular size, even if you're layering it, in a crewneck and soft merino wool.

### The Ties

No tie in your closet should be wider than 3" at its widest point, or have a solid sheen (à la Regis). Instead, opt for a muted tone with texture or small printed patterns. Or consider the power of the knit tie.

### Black Cap-Toe Oxfords

They go great with just about any suit you own.

### Desert Boots

More dressed up than a sneaker but not as stuffy as a leather oxford.

### Boots

A refined pair of leather work boots can still look dressed up.

# THE FATHER AND SON (AND MOM) WHO BRAVED THE ELEMENTS

Wilbert "Bill" Gore was a chemical engineer who started with his wife, Vieve, W. L. Gore & Associates in the family's basement in 1958 in Delaware. They were making ribbon cables for computer companies. The chemical engineering bug ran in the family. The couple's son, Bob, who had a PhD in the field, joined the company in 1963. It was in 1969 when the younger Gore, experimenting with polytetrafluoroethylene (PTFE) that he expanded the material to create what would become known as GORE-TEX. The discovered material would wind up in all kinds of applications, but the most common is its fabric form which, thanks to the Gore family, waterproofs our winter boots and coats.

# THE BARBERSHOP RITUAL

There are two ways to experience the barbershop. Each has its merits.

You can treat it like car maintenance: perfunctory, utilitarian, in and out, minimal fuss, know what you're getting, every four weeks, give or take. You walk in, wait your turn, ask for a guard number on the sides and a little off the top. Hand the guy twenty bucks and you're on your way.

Or you can treat it like a spa experience: luxuriate, relax, chitchat, and finesse your look. You'll pay a little more, but you get the treatment in the chair, a hot towel, a hot shave to the back of the neck, and a quiet consultation that acknowledges, but doesn't make insecure, the thinning of your hair.

In either event though, tip. Always tip.

# SHAVING: THE IDEAL PROCESS

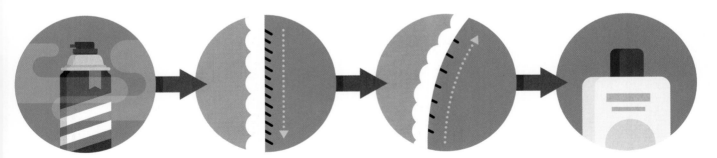

If you shower before you shave, apply the cream right before you get out of the shower. The steam and moisture will help fatten and soften your whiskers. If not, apply cream to wet skin and let sit for two minutes.

With a fresh blade, shave in the direction of the grain of your whiskers, pulling your skin taut with your thumb from above the blade.

For hard to reach spots, reapply cream and go against the grain.

Rinse with cold water, pat your skin dry, and apply a post-shave cream. Avoid alcohol-heavy aftershave.

103

# THREE TIE KNOTS YOU SHOULD KNOW

## THE FOUR-IN-HAND

For just about any style of shirt collar and width of tie. Especially good for knit ties.

1. With the wide end of the tie on your right, let the skinny end of the tie hang higher, above your belly button. Cross the wide end over the left and pass it under the skinny end of the tie, so the back of the tie is facing out.

2. Bring the wide end of the tie across the front of the skinny end again, and bring it around.

3. Now, bring the wide end through the loop around your neck, and pull it through the loop you just created in the front.

4. Tighten and adjust by pulling the knot up and the wide end of the tie down.

 **A NOTE ON THE BOW TIE**

Unless you're an English professor from the 1950s, the bow tie should be occasioned for the most formal events. Say, the wedding of one of your children, or if you get invited to a state dinner. And if you're going to wear one, avoid the clip-on.

## THE HALF WINDSOR

For spread-collared shirts and ties that are of a lighter to medium material. It's slightly more formal than the Four-in-Hand.

1. Like the Four-in-Hand, start with the wide end of the tie on your right, and let the skinny end of the tie hang higher, above your belly button. Cross the wide end over the left and pass it under the skinny end of the tie, so the back of the tie is facing out.

2. Now, pass the wide end over and through the loop around your neck near the center, and pull it through to the left.

3. Bring the wide end of the tie right across the front of the skinny end again.

4. Pull the wide end up through the neck loop again, and this time, pull it through the small loop you created closer to the front.

5. Tighten the knot and adjust.

## THE FULL WINDSOR

Spread-collared shirts. And for making a power statement. This fella's big.

1. Again, start with the wide end of the tie on your right, and let the skinny end of the tie hang higher, above your belly button. This time, cross the wide end over the left, pass it under the skinny end of the tie, and now pull the wide end up and through the neck loop, down to the left.

2. Bring the wide end around the back and to the right of the skinny end.

3. Bring the wide end up and through the neck loop, then down to the right.

4. Cross the wide end across the front again, then bring it up through the neck loop and down through the front loop you just created.

5. Tighten the knot and adjust.

**1**

Have a spray bottle of water handy and set your iron to its highest setting. Use the water to saturate any stubborn wrinkles and iron them out.

**2**

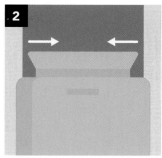

Unfold the collar, laying it flat on the ironing board. Working from the ends of the collar into the center, move the iron in a firm, circular motion.

**3**

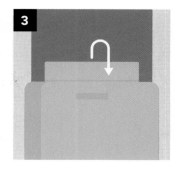

Fold the collar back down and give it a light press.

**4**

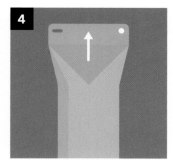

Unbutton your cuffs and lay one flat on the ironing board, ironing from inside the cuff. Do the other cuff.

**5**

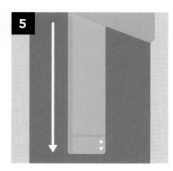

Lay the sleeve flat on the ironing board and work your way from the shoulder down. Flip over and do the other side of the sleeve. Flip the shirt and do the same to the opposite sleeve. Don't put too much pressure on the edges of the sleeve—you don't want a drastic crease.

**6**

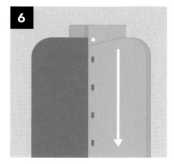

Over the squared end of the ironing board, lay one open half of the front of the shirt, with the neck of the shirt at the end of the board. Work from the neck and shoulder down. Saturate the button plackets with water, pull the shirt taut, and follow the plackets straight down with the iron. Do the other side.

**7**

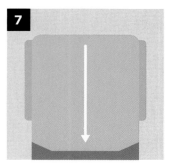

Flip the shirt over, draping the middle of the shirt over the back, squared-off end of the ironing board, and gently iron from the top down in light, circular motions.

**8**

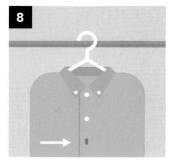

Hang on a hanger to cool, with the top two buttons fastened.

FOR THE LAZY DAD

Take it to the cleaners.

# THE
# WHEN AND WHERE OF THE POLO SHIRT

CASUAL

Baseball Game

Kid's Soccer Game

Grocery Store

INAPPROPRIATE

Graduation Party

APPROPRIATE

Job Interview

Golf Course

Anniversary Party

The Office

Office Barbecue

Steakhouse

DRESSY

1889
1917
1928
1930s

# A BRIEF HISTORY OF THE CARHARTT CHORE COAT

In 1889, Hamilton Carhartt & Company began a manufacturing operation in Detroit, Michigan, making workwear for rail workers, including bib overalls. In 1917 the company put out its first ad for a Chore Coat, with its distinctive four front pockets. In 1928, the jacket was first produced in duck cloth, the fabric that most of us recognize it in today. In the 1930s, Carhartt added the distinctive corduroy collar and blanket linings for warmth. It's been the go-to jacket for working men ever since, one worn by every stripe of dad—be it for hunting, camping, tailgating, stringing holiday decorations, or just looking damn good while running errands.

## THE BIG FAT WALLET

There was a time when you had video rental store membership cards and coffee shop punch loyalty cards. A time when you carried cash on a regular basis, asked for and kept receipts. And so you needed a storage center big enough for all your crap. The Costanza-ifying of our wallets is no longer a reality as our cards move to our phones, our receipts get e-mailed, and photos of the kids live in the cloud. Nowadays, a simple card carrier loaded with a debit card, credit card, license, and a couple twenties will do the trick. Our backs are thankful for it.

**FOSSILS OF FATHERHOOD**

THE WHEN AND WHERE OF

# SOCK STYLES

## WHITE

With athletic shoes. Preferably of the tennis variety. Permissible with jeans. Never with any kind of dress pant.

## BLACK

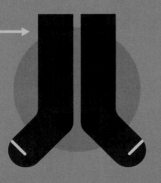

With black shoes. And black, charcoal, or gray pants. Never with khakis. At funerals, job interviews, weddings, or more formal events.

## NO-SHOW

With running shoes. Or dress shoes, if you're going for a more fashionable, show off the ankle move. Just make sure they, you know, don't show.

## ARGYLE, PATTERNED, COLORED

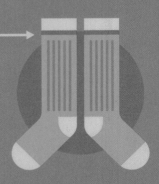

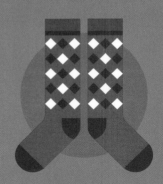

With brown or black dress shoes, boots, and your dressier sneakers. Permissible with every kind of pant. Use to imbue your outfit with more personality, but don't lean on a statement sock to make you more interesting. That's up to you alone.

## NONE

With no shoes or flip-flops. Only on the beach. Lest you want to risk stinking up not only your shoes, but also your entire home.

# AN HEIRLOOM WATCH

## BUYING

When the time comes to celebrate a milestone—a wedding, the birth of a child, a big promotion—and you have the funds, opt for a fine mechanical watch. One with classic design details that will age well. Something like the Rolex Oyster Perpetual Submariner. Or the OMEGA Speedmaster (it's the watch the astronauts wore to the moon). You want something that doesn't look too elegant—you want to be able to wear it most days. Go to an authorized dealer or jeweler, keep all your paperwork, and insure the watch.

## RECEIVING

Thank your father for the thoughtfulness. Promise to take good care of it—and do so! (see below)—and that you'll share it, and its story, with your kids. A thank-you note saying as much after helps, too.

## MAINTAINING

Schedule regular maintenance with the watch manufacturer about every ten years. Most offer services through their dealers. And show it off to the kids. Build their interest in it, so when it comes time for the watch to become theirs, they have a sense of its history and meaning to you.

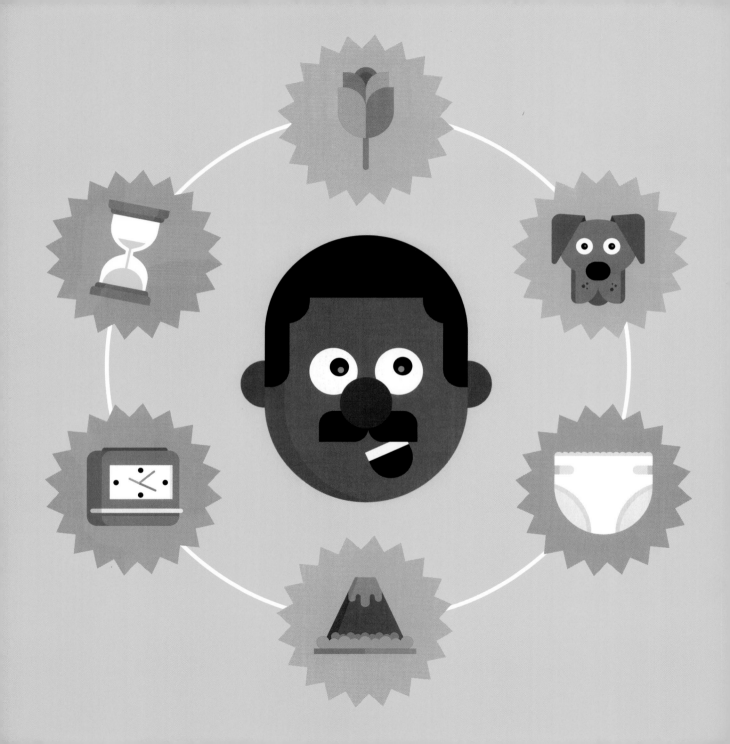

# WISDOM

# GOLDEN RETRIEVER

| | |
|---|---|
| **PRO** | Friendly and affectionate and loyal. The ultimate dog traits. |
| **CON** | Requires a lot of activity and tends to bark. |

# BRUSSELS GRIFFON

| | |
|---|---|
| **PRO** | Sized for small homes and families. Pugnacious and energetic. |
| **CON** | Not great with separation. Or at roughhousing with kids. |

# MUTT

| | |
|---|---|
| **PRO** | No weird inbred diseases or traits. Unique looking! |
| **CON** | You don't know what you're getting on the temperament or trainability side. |

# THE RIGHT DOG FOR EVERY FAMILY

# BULLDOG

| | |
|---|---|
| **PRO** | Loyal and comfortable in the city or in a rural home. |
| **CON** | Have a tendency to chew things up. And their snub noses affect their breathing. |

# BEAGLE

| | |
|---|---|
| **PRO** | Easygoing and good in big groups. |
| **CON** | Sheds, requires lots of exercise, can wander off when latching on to a scent. |

# LABRADOR RETRIEVER

| | |
|---|---|
| **PRO** | Quiet, friendly, and easy to train. |
| **CON** | They're shedders and require a lot of activity. |

FIDO

# NAMING YOUR DOG

First, make sure it's something that you're comfortable yelling for the neighbors to hear. "Here, Cookie!" is embarrassing for everyone. Including the dog. As fun as human names might be, they can be confusing, and a little offensive when you introduce human Justin to dog Justin. Personality traits should inform naming over physical appearance. Let the kids take a stab at it and put it up to a vote. Don't discount the classics. Rex. Spot. Pepper. Petey. Spike. Sprocket. All viable dog names.

# THE
# COMPLAINTS

A truncated list of dad whines.

FROM THE DESK OF DAD

The price of gas

The price of movie tickets

The price of everything

Lights left on in any room

"Those bozos in Congress"

Junk mail, especially catalogs

All head coaches

Social media (until the kids show them how to do it)

"Noise" or "racket"

Barking dogs

FROM THE DESK OF DAD

Traffic

Potholes

Speed traps

Late newspaper delivery

Too much ice

Not enough ice

Time others spend in the shower

Time others spend getting dressed

Line-cutting

"Eyesores" (i.e., lawns needing cut, houses needing painted, cars needing washed, etc.)

# THE CALM, COOL, COLLECTED COLLEGE DROP-OFF

Former president Barack Obama said of dropping off his eldest daughter, Malia, at Harvard in 2017 that it was like open-heart surgery. He called it "a reminder that, at the end of our lives, whatever else we've accomplished, the things that we'll remember are the joys that our children—and hopefully way later, our grandchildren—bring us."

So, how do you keep the tears at bay? Make yourself useful, but not intrusive. Pick small, simple projects around the dorm room, like cutting out cabinet liners or assembling some Ikea furniture. Focus yourself on the project at hand. You've already done all the work to get them to this point. You've got to trust that you've prepared them well enough. Then, when you're in the car, you can sob. Wait to text until the next day.

## HOW TO ▶ HAGGLE

|  |  |  |  | 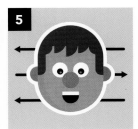 |
|---|---|---|---|---|
| **1** Talk second. That is, defer to the party offering up the item to put a price out there first. | **2** Say, "hmmm". Furrow your brow. Make it look like you're thinking it over. | **3** Stay quiet. See if the seller will bargain himself down first. | **4** Then offer the lowest end of what you'd pay without screwing over the seller. | **5** Go back and forth until you're at a place you're happy with. You want everyone to win here. |

# WHAT THE
# FLOWERS YOU GIVE MEAN

Giving flowers to someone is a thoughtful gesture, sure. But not all blooms express the same sentiment. Turns out there's a meaning and occasion behind most bouquets. Here's what you need to know to be the most thoughtful man you can be.

## FOR
## APOLOGIES

 PURPLE HYACINTH

The symbolic meaning of these says: "Please forgive me"

## FOR
## THE HOLIDAYS

 RED POINSETTIA

 AMARYLLIS

## FOR
## MOTHER'S DAY

 PINK CARNATIONS

They symbolize a mother's love

## FOR
## GET WELL SOON

 MARIGOLDS

 YELLOW TULIPS

They're meant to be cheerful (and they don't have much of a smell, which is good for the sick)

FOR
# ROMANCE

 RED ROSES (Love)

 PINK ROSES (Passion)

 YELLOW ROSES (Friendship)

 WHITE ROSES (Purity)

FOR
# DISSAPOINTMENT

 YELLOW CARNATIONS

For when you're trying to send someone
an underhanded message

FOR
# FUNERALS

 CALLA LILIES

 CHRYSANTHEMUMS

 ROSES

White or blue signify peace and humility;
red or orange celebrate the life of the departed

FOR
# NEW BEGINNINGS

 DAFFODILS

 DAISIES

# $233,610

Average cost of raising a kid through the age of 17

# $422

How much the average parent spends per child on holiday presents

Average cost to charter and insure a Little League team

# $6

PER PLAYER

| Average Tooth Fairy payout | $1 |
| Number of baby teeth a kid loses | 20 |

Total Tooth Fairy Expenses

# $20

PER KID

## THE ECONOMICS OF
# BEING A DAD

# 2,700

How many diapers a baby will go through in its first year

# 27%

Households with children under 18 where only the father works

# 32.2

Hours per week the average dad spends on household chores and childcare

Fathers tend to be
# PAID MORE
than childless men

* sourced from data released between 2014 and 2018

# HOW TO GET A SMALL CHILD TO SMILE AT A CAMERA

**When saying "Say, cheese" isn't enough.**

You've seen the routine at your local mall's portrait studio: high-pitched gasps from a photographer, waving a stuffed animal at a dazed child propped up on a carpeted apple box. It's because it works. Sometimes. What also works:

1. Say their name, like you're surprised to see them. "There's Sally!" They'll be delighted.

2. Have them hide their face, like a game of peek-a-boo. Then when they look up and see you, snap the photo.

3. The oddest sounds you can think of, just before pressing the shutter. Like monkey-sounding "Ooh-ooh, ah-ahs!"

(No one said you were going to look good.)

## THE PHOTO ALBUM

**FOSSILS OF FATHERHOOD**

Sure, you've got plenty of photos of the kids on your phone. They're probably your background. But what's missing is that old black-and-white snapshot of your Uncle Art, who may or may not have been, uh, connected, nursing a steinie beer bottle at a checked-tablecloth-cloaked table and looking dapper in a fedora and pinstripe three-piece suit. That picture is sitting in an album up on a shelf in Grandpa's house. What with all our photos having gone digital, pulling that album off the shelf, or filling one up, is all the less likely. And with it the chance to tell your kids about who Uncle Art was and why men always dressed so sharp back in the day.

# THE
# VOLCANO SCHOOL PROJECT

How to make the classic scientific demonstration of . . . making a mess.

# MATERIALS

## FOR THE VOLCANO

- A firm piece of cardboard or plywood as a base
- Newspaper cut into long strips
- Several pieces of balled-up newspaper
- A water bottle with the top cut off
- Papier-mâché mixture
  (one part water to one part flour)

## FOR THE VOLCANO

- ¼ cup water
- ¼ cup white vinegar
- 3 drops dish soap
- 3 drops red food coloring
- 1 tbsp baking soda
- 1 sheet toilet paper

# CONSTRUCTION

**1** Attach your base to water bottle with glue or tape. Then tape the balled-up newspaper around the bottle to build the shape of the volcano.

**2** Dip the long strips of newspaper into the papier-mâché mixture, removing excess paste with your fingers, and applying the strips to the volcano. Continue to layer on the strips until you've created the final shape of the volcano.

**3** Allow to dry overnight. Then paint the volcano.

# ERUPTION

**1** Mix the water, vinegar, dish soap, and food coloring, and decant the mixture into the water bottle at the center of the volcano.

**2** Pile the baking soda onto the square of toilet paper and twist up the ends.

**3** Drop the packet of baking soda into the volcano and let it spew.

# HOW TO
# STAY IN TOUCH WITH OLD FRIENDS

## LET TECH BE YOUR GUIDE

It's easier than ever now, between social media and the immediacy and ease of texting. Taking the onus off a one-to-one interaction and open up a group chat or an e-mail thread with your old high school crew. Chime in when there's news to report. It doesn't have to be daily, or even monthly. But knowing the thread is there, and can always be picked up, makes ongoing communication easiest.

## FANTASY SPORTS OR VIDEO GAMES

You probably originally bonded with these people over a shared activity. Bridge the gaps in geography by bringing your shared interests online. While you're playing Call of Duty with your college roommates, you can catch each other up on your lives, wives, and kids, and blow off some steam like old times. Or connect over a fantasy league. The weekly trade deadlines offer ample opportunity for the kind of ribbing you guys are used to.

## PLAN A TRIP

If you've been catching up online, over e-mail, or texting, propose getting everyone together again in person. Pick a central location, or somewhere near the hometown where you all grew up. And when you finally see each other in person, try not to look too shocked over how much hair you've both lost or weight you've both put on.

# GIVE A TOAST FOR ANY OCCASION

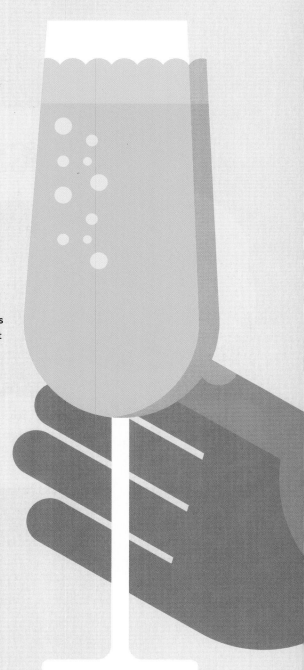

First, this should be fun and easy! If it's a celebratory occasion and you're surrounded by people you like, if not love, whatever you have to say will be appreciated and listened to. You're likely giving a toast to show your appreciation or share you excitement. People love that. So no need to be nervous.

Make sure your drink is at least three quarters full. If this is an impromptu ordeal, take a minute to figure out what you want to express to the crowd—gratitude, awe, congratulations. Now, stand up and get people's attention. Shouting is allowed, if clinking the glass doesn't work first. If you're being introduced, thank the person who's brought you up to speak. And thank the hosts of the event.

Hold your glass at chest height. The general rule is that if your arm is getting tired, it's time to wrap it up. State your remarks about how thrilled you are for whatever the occasion is. If there's a (short!) anecdote or story off the top of your head that reflects the significance of the occasion or the person being honored, tell it. It can be funny, but don't make fun of people. Make fun of only yourself, but don't be too self-deprecating. There's a want to often end on a quote, but that's cliché. Instead, just end with a raising of your glass and a robust: "Here's to you!"

# "THE TALKS"

## DRUGS

Use a car ride—captive audience—to start the conversation. And remember, it's a conversation. Not a lecture. Open with an anecdote, like an insight from an article you read about the opioid epidemic, or the legalization of weed in a state. Ask them what they think of that. Lay out the dangers of drug use. What it does to their young brain. And how you understand they might feel pressure to partake. Ask them what kind of life they'd like for themselves, and how drugs can be an impediment to that. Let them know you're available to talk if they need to.

## DEATH

Whether it's the death of a grandparent or a beloved pet, the first conversation with your kids about death is never easy. Bring it up gently: "Sweetheart, I have some sad news . . ." They are going to have a lot of questions. Do your best to answer them in a way that is both reassuring and honest. You don't want to scare them, but you don't want to lie to them, either. When they are grown, you'll want to have a frank discussion over end-of-life plans. Again, introduce it gently: "If something should happen . . ." It's not a conversation they'll want to have, no matter how old they are. Some tears will likely be shed over the thought that you'll one day be gone. Reassure them that you're bringing it up because you love them and want them to be prepared.

# SEX

Might sound weird, but this should be an ongoing conversation starting when they're young. Begin by identifying body parts, so that it's not awkward later when you begin using words like "penis" in more complex ways. If a kid asks about babies, explain the simple biology—they're still a few years off from grasping the big picture. A one-off sit-down is ultimately not all that useful except for heaping on embarrassment for both of you. During middle school years as they reach their early teens (and before any boyfriends or girlfriends start coming around), start discussions about STDs and protection. Ask your kids what they would have done in situations and what they think about those things. If your kid brings up questions about sex with you, answer them. Don't say "Ask your mother." That response implies shame or embarrassment.

# DIVORCE

If it's the last thing you and your soon-to-be former spouse do together, it should be this. The two of you need to plan what you're going to tell the kids, and how you're going to tell them. Call a family meeting, and get everyone in the room together. Try to check your own emotions, and level with the kids: "Mom and Dad have had a hard time, and it's just not working." Assure them that it's not their fault, let them know that they're great kids. Be open to questions from them, and don't freak out if their questions come off as selfish. Listen to their reaction, recognize it's valid, and accept it—how they react is how they react, whether that's seeking a hug from you or hiding in their room.

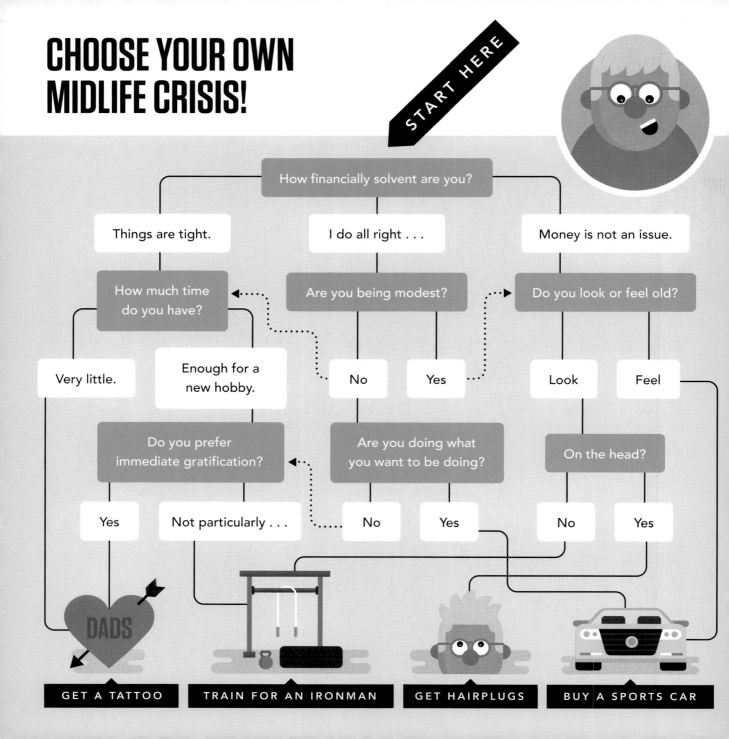

# GREATEST MOMENT IN ALL OF DAD HISTORY

# THE BIRTH OF YOUR KID

Because none of this matters
until they're here.